FOR DUMMIES™

BESTSELLING
BOOK SERIES

The Triathlete's Training Diary For Dummies®

Cheat Sheet

Sample Diary

Training Goals
Goals!

Train for Tri One on 5/27
Work up to half-marathon distance
Improve swimming efficiency

Date: 4/2

Training	Time/Distance	Sets	Reps
Bike ride	57 min/15 miles		
Run	27 min/3 miles		

Food for Thought
Need to smooth transition between bike and run

Date: 4/3

Training	Time/Distance	Sets	Reps
Weights			
Squats		3	10
Hamstring cur_		3	8
Calf raise		2	10

D0957315

Food for Thoug_
Worked on staying streamlined in water

Personal Triathlon Bests

Swimming	Time/Date	Time/Date	Time/Date
100 yards			
400 yards			
800 yards			

Cycling	Time/Date	Time/Date	Time/Date
5 miles			
10 miles			
25 miles			
50K (31 miles)			
50 miles			
100K (62 miles)			
100 miles			
112 miles			

Running	Time/Date	Time/Date	Time/Date
1 mile			
2 miles			
5K (3.1 miles)			
10K (6.2 miles)			
Half marathon			
Marathon			

Triathlon Race Day Checklist

- ❑ Sweats
- ❑ Sunglasses
- ❑ Hat
- ❑ Sunscreen
- ❑ Watch
- ❑ Heart-rate monitor
- ❑ Swim goggles
- ❑ Wetsuit

- ❑ Spare tube/tire pump
- ❑ Safety pins (for your number)
- ❑ Money
- ❑ Change
- ❑ Identification
- ❑ Change of clothes
- ❑ Change of shoes

IDG BOOKS WORLDWIDE

For Dummies™: Bestselling Book Series for Beginners

The Triathlete's Training Diary
FOR DUMMIES®

by Allen St. John

IDG Books Worldwide, Inc.
An International Data Group Company

Foster City, CA ✦ Chicago, IL ✦ Indianapolis, IN ✦ New York, NY

The Triathlete's Training Diary For Dummies®

Published by
IDG Books Worldwide, Inc.
An International Data Group Company
909 Third Avenue
New York, NY 10022
www.idgbooks.com (IDG Books Worldwide Web Site)
www.dummies.com (Dummies Press Web Site)

Library of Congress Control Number: 00-110908

ISBN: 0-7645-5339-9

Printed in the United States of America

10 9 8 7 6 5 4 3 2 1

1O/RT/QS/QR/IN

Distributed in the United States by IDG Books Worldwide, Inc.

Distributed by CDG Books Canada Inc. for Canada; by Transworld Publishers Limited in the United Kingdom; by IDG Norge Books for Norway; by IDG Sweden Books for Sweden; by IDG Books Australia Publishing Corporation Pty. Ltd. for Australia and New Zealand; by TransQuest Publishers Pte Ltd. for Singapore, Malaysia, Thailand, Indonesia, and Hong Kong; by Gotop Information Inc. for Taiwan; by ICG Muse, Inc. for Japan; by Intersoft for South Africa; by Eyrolles for France; by International Thomson Publishing for Germany, Austria, and Switzerland; by Distribuidora Cuspide for Argentina; by LR International for Brazil; by Galileo Libros for Chile; by Ediciones ZETA S.C.R. Ltda. for Peru; by WS Computer Publishing Corporation, Inc., for the Philippines; by Contemporanea de Ediciones for Venezuela; by Express Computer Distributors for the Caribbean and West Indies; by Micronesia Media Distributor, Inc. for Micronesia; by Chips Computadoras S.A. de C.V. for Mexico; by Editorial Norma de Panama S.A. for Panama; by American Bookshops for Finland.

For general information on IDG Books Worldwide's books in the U.S., please call our Consumer Customer Service department at 800-762-2974. For reseller information, including discounts and premium sales, please call our Reseller Customer Service department at 800-434-3422.

For information on where to purchase IDG Books Worldwide's books outside the U.S., please contact our International Sales department at 317-572-3993 or fax 317-572-4002.

For consumer information on foreign language translations, please contact our Customer Service department at 1-800-434-3422, fax 317-572-4002, or e-mail rights@idgbooks.com.

For information on licensing foreign or domestic rights, please phone +1-650-653-7098.

For sales inquiries and special prices for bulk quantities, please contact our Order Services department at 800-434-4322 or write to the address above.

For information on using IDG Books Worldwide's books in the classroom or for ordering examination copies, please contact our Educational Sales department at 800-434-2086 or fax 317-572-4005.

For press review copies, author interviews, or other publicity information, please contact our Public Relations department at 650-653-7000 or fax 650-653-7500.

For authorization to photocopy items for corporate, personal, or educational use, please contact Copyright Clearance Center, 222 Rosewood Drive, Danvers, MA 01923, or fax 978-750-4470.

is a registered trademark under exclusive license to IDG Books Worldwide, Inc., from International Data Group, Inc.

About the Author

Allen St. John is the author of *Bicycling For Dummies* and *Skiing For Dummies* and is a former senior editor at *Conde Nast Women's Sports and Fitness* magazine. An avid recreational athlete, he has written about sports and fitness for a wide variety of national newspapers and magazines including *Men's Journal, MH-18, U.S. News & World Report, Maxim,* and the *New York Times.* He's a columnist for *Skiing* magazine, a regular contributor to *Tennis,* and a founding contributing editor for *Bike,* and he has covered the New York Yankees for the *Village Voice* for the past eight seasons, as well as contributed to the hardcover book and CD-ROM, *The Way Baseball Works.* He lives in Upper Montclair, New Jersey, with his wife, Sally, and two children, Ethan and Emma.

ABOUT IDG BOOKS WORLDWIDE

Welcome to the world of IDG Books Worldwide.

IDG Books Worldwide, Inc., is a subsidiary of International Data Group, the world's largest publisher of computer-related information and the leading global provider of information services on information technology. IDG was founded more than 30 years ago by Patrick J. McGovern and now employs more than 9,000 people worldwide. IDG publishes more than 290 computer publications in over 75 countries. More than 90 million people read one or more IDG publications each month.

Launched in 1990, IDG Books Worldwide is today the #1 publisher of best-selling computer books in the United States. We are proud to have received eight awards from the Computer Press Association in recognition of editorial excellence and three from Computer Currents' First Annual Readers' Choice Awards. Our best-selling ...For Dummies® series has more than 50 million copies in print with translations in 31 languages. IDG Books Worldwide, through a joint venture with IDG's Hi-Tech Beijing, became the first U.S. publisher to publish a computer book in the People's Republic of China. In record time, IDG Books Worldwide has become the first choice for millions of readers around the world who want to learn how to better manage their businesses.

Our mission is simple: Every one of our books is designed to bring extra value and skill-building instructions to the reader. Our books are written by experts who understand and care about our readers. The knowledge base of our editorial staff comes from years of experience in publishing, education, and journalism — experience we use to produce books to carry us into the new millennium. In short, we care about books, so we attract the best people. We devote special attention to details such as audience, interior design, use of icons, and illustrations. And because we use an efficient process of authoring, editing, and desktop publishing our books electronically, we can spend more time ensuring superior content and less time on the technicalities of making books.

You can count on our commitment to deliver high-quality books at competitive prices on topics you want to read about. At IDG Books Worldwide, we continue in the IDG tradition of delivering quality for more than 30 years. You'll find no better book on a subject than one from IDG Books Worldwide.

John J. Kilcullen

John Kilcullen
Chairman and CEO
IDG Books Worldwide, Inc.

*Eighth Annual
Computer Press
Awards ➪1992*

*Ninth Annual
Computer Press
Awards ➪1993*

*Tenth Annual
Computer Press
Awards ➪1994*

*Eleventh Annual
Computer Press
Awards ➪1995*

Dedication

To my kids, Ethan and Emma, who do everything they can to keep me in shape.

Author's Acknowledgments

Although there's one name on the cover, a book is a team effort. I'd like to thank everyone at IDG Books, including executive editor, Stacy Collins, and project editors, Mike Kelly and Greg Summers, and of course my agent, the incomparable Mark Reiter, and the rest of the good people at IMG Literary. Special thanks goes to this book's technical reviewer, Jeff Csatari, who helped make sure that the information in this book is as smart and accurate as it can be.

Thanks also to all the editors who help me make a living putting words together, including James Kaminsky, Albert Baime, and Alex Straus at *Maxim,* David Sparrow, James Martin, and Bill Gray at *Tennis,* Rick Kahl, Helen Olsson, Bevin Wallace, Mike Miracle, and Charlie Glass at *Skiing,* Dana White at *Teen People,* Brian Duffy at *U.S. News & World Report,* King Kaufman at *Salon.com,* Jerry Beilinson at *National Geographic Adventure,* Miles Seligman at the *Village Voice,* Michael Anderson at the *New York Times Book Review,* Jack Schwartz at the *New York Times,* Kyle Creighton at the *New York Times Magazine,* and, of course, anyone that I'm forgetting.

And finally to my wife, Sally, my support, my inspiration, and my best friend.

Publisher's Acknowledgments

We're proud of this book; please send us your comments through our IDG Books Worldwide Online Registration Form located at www.dummies.com

Some of the people who helped bring this book to market include the following:

Acquisitions, Editorial, and Media Development

Project Editor: Michael Kelly

Executive Editor: Stacy S. Collins

Copy Editor: Robert Annis

Acquisitions Coordinator: Stacy Klein

General Reviewer: Jeff Csatari

Editorial Manager: Jennifer Ehrlich

Editorial Administrator: Michelle Hacker

Cover Photos: Stone/Will Curtis; Joe Patronite/Image Bank

Production

Project Coordinator: Emily Wichlinski

Layout and Graphics: Amy Adrian, Sean Decker, LeAndra Johnson, Julia Trippetti, Erin Zeltner

Proofreaders: Laura Albert, John Bitter, York Production Services, Inc.

Indexer: York Production Services, Inc.

General and Administrative

IDG Books Worldwide, Inc.: John Kilcullen, CEO; Bill Barry, President and COO; John Ball, Executive VP, Operations & Administration; John Harris, CFO

IDG Books Consumer Reference Group

Business: Kathleen A. Welton, Vice President and Publisher; Kevin Thornton, Acquisitions Manager

Cooking/Gardening: Jennifer Feldman, Associate Vice President and Publisher

Education/Reference: Diane Graves Steele, Vice President and Publisher; Greg Tubach, Publishing Director

Lifestyles: Kathleen Nebenhaus, Vice President and Publisher; Tracy Boggier, Managing Editor

Pets: Dominique De Vito, Associate Vice President and Publisher; Tracy Boggier, Managing Editor

Travel: Michael Spring, Vice President and Publisher; Suzanne Jannetta, Editorial Director; Brice Gosnell, Managing Editor

IDG Books Consumer Editorial Services: Kathleen Nebenhaus, Vice President and Publisher; Kristin A. Cocks, Editorial Director; Cindy Kitchel, Editorial Director

IDG Books Consumer Production: Debbie Stailey, Production Director

IDG Books Packaging: Marc J. Mikulich, Vice President, Brand Strategy and Research

◆

The publisher would like to give special thanks to Patrick J. McGovern, without whom this book would not have been possible.

◆

Contents at a Glance

Cartoons at a Glance

By Rich Tennant

"Listen, thanks. I'll return them as soon as I get the wheels fixed."

page 61

page 7

"I heard it was good to cross-train, so I'm mixing my weight training with scuba diving."

page 181

Cartoon Information:
Fax: 978-546-7747
E-Mail: richtennant@the5thwave.com
World Wide Web: www.the5thwave.com

Table of Contents

Introduction

•••

Swim. Ride. Run. What could be simpler than running a triathlon? Or harder? It's more than just an event; it's a way to test your limits. When you get to the starting line, you'll find that today's sweat pays dividends when you cross the tape. This book is about helping you toward those oh-wow moments when you find yourself able to do something that you never could before.

About This Book

So you've decided to hide that bowl of nacho chips, pop the AAA batteries out of the remote, and get off the couch for good. Congratulations. But while that first step is important, the real key to getting in shape — and staying there — is consistency. Day after day, week after week, month after month, you need to make exercise as much a part of your day as brushing your teeth. And that's where this book comes in.

Part information source, part motivational tool, and part journal, this book will help you get started exercising, help you to get the most out of every workout, and, yes, even supply a gentle kick in the pants when your willpower flags. Not bad for a pile of paper that fits in your gym bag.

In these pages, you find out how to set up an exercise program that's just right for you. You discover how to warm up properly to prevent injuries. You get a wealth of workout tips in a variety of popular workout activities, from walking to swimming to in-line skating. Finally, you find out about how to cool down and recharge for your next workout.

And then comes the part of the book that you write yourself. The meat of this book is a customizable workout log where you can list your personal goals and record your progress. It's this section that makes this book truly *your* book.

And finally, because everyone loves a list, the Part of Tens, which gives you a few more tips and even a couple of jokes.

Why You Should Log Your Workouts

First, here's what you shouldn't expect from this book. It won't improve your penmanship. It won't win you a Pulitzer Prize. And unless you win, say, a Nobel Prize or a presidential election on your own, it won't provide an insight into your personality for biographers of a future generation.

What logging your workouts does give you is pretty simple: motivation and information. First the motivation part. Have you ever made a to-do list? Have you ever made a to-do list after you've already completed the first three tasks, just so you get the satisfaction of crossing them off? Admit it, it's a great feeling. That's the same kind of reward that's waiting for you at the end of every exercise session.

The great thing about fitness is that it's quantifiable. Practice your new arrangement of "Afternoon Delight" on your Casiotone for a month, and you're depending on your friends to tell you how much better you sound. But when it comes to fitness, you're not dependent on the kindness of strangers. All you need to do is flip back through your training diary and realize that you're going farther and faster, or lifting more, than you did a month ago. Trust me, that's also a great feeling.

But unlike your old to-do lists, the completed pages of this training diary will also contain plenty of vital information. You'll see which goals were easy and fun to attain, and which goals made you feel like Wile E. Coyote chasing the Road Runner. By reviewing your entries, you'll be able to detect personal patterns and tendencies that will allow you to train more efficiently in the future. You'll also be able to improve your performance and prevent injuries. And, finally, you'll be able to have more fun . . . beyond the simple joy of seeing your accomplishments immortalized in black and white.

How to Use Your Training Diary

The first thing you need to use your training diary is a pen. Got it? Good. The next thing you need is a plan. Before you start keeping a training diary, you should have a basic idea of what your fitness goals are and how to achieve them. (Don't worry, I talk about all that in Chapter 1.)

The next thing you need is a willingness to make your training diary your new friend. Bring this book with you to the gym, keeping it in your gym bag right next to your shower shoes. Or if you exercise outdoors, set it down on the kitchen counter, right next to a bottle of Gatorade, and make a bee-line for it as soon as you get back from an exercise session. As soon as you've completed a workout, make it a habit to write down what you did and how you felt. If you record your workout right away, it's easy and fun. If you wait until later, it becomes a hassle. Or doesn't get done at all.

At the minimum, you should record how long you worked out, how many reps at each weight you did in the weight room, or the duration and distance of your aerobic workout. You might also record how you felt when you got up and before, during, and after your workout.

Because I know you're busy, this diary doesn't assume that you're going to work out every day of every week — in fact, a good workout plan includes a healthy balance of exercise and rest. With the diary section, you can track your progress over a ten-day stretch, customizing your journal each day for whatever workout you choose, running, weight training, and so on. And you can use the Training Goals section to write down your personal training goals and the Workout Wrap-Up section to celebrate your training accomplishments.

Finally, don't forget the Food for Thought section to track your diet and nutrition goals, as well as how you felt during your workout and what you should focus on for your next training session.

But this isn't a police report — your training diary can include anything that you feel is important. Did "99 Luftbaloons" keep running through your head on your bike ride? Did you finally figure out mid-rep why Ginger brought all those dresses for a three-hour tour? Did you step on the scale after your shower and finally see the needle settle at your target weight? Then write it down.

Cheater, Cheater, Biscotti Eater

"When you cheat, you're only cheating yourself." Bet you haven't heard that one since grammar school. Well, I'm hear to tell you that Mrs. Moloney was right — about that, not about the fact that you'll never amount to anything unless you sit up straighter at your desk.

So while it's very tempting to write in on that first line — ran 7 miles / 42 minutes or bench press: 225 pounds — don't do it unless you really did it. First off, remember that this is a diary. And like the one with the poodle fur and the tiny gold key in which you promised your undying love to Jimmy Whatshisname, it's completely private. Your little sister won't read it unless you show it to her, so there's no need to hide it under the bed. Unless you decide to share it with your friends — or leave it for your biographer — no one's going to be impressed by what you wrote down, or think less of you if your workout was kind of lame.

So if you don't complete your planned workout on any given day, that's okay. Write down what you did and, if you can, why you think you fell short of your goal. Too tired? Too sore? Too little time? That info will help you down the road.

If you skip a couple of days of working out, that's okay, too. But if you start fudging and writing down miles not run and weights not lifted, you won't have an accurate yardstick of what you really did and how fast you really progressed. When you go back a couple of months later, you'll feel like a special prosecutor, trying to piece together who did what when. So take some sage advice from Samuel Langhorne Clemens — "When in doubt, tell the truth." Somewhere down the road, you'll be glad you did.

How This Book Is Organized

Okay, this isn't *Anna Karenina* and I don't expect you to sit down with a bottle of vodka and a box of tissues and read it from start to finish. But this book does have a beginning, middle, and end. First off, you get a bit of sage advice. In the opening chapters, you find out how this book is organized — in fact that's what you're doing right now — how to plan a workout program, how to warm up properly, how to get the most out of your workout, and how to cool down and refuel for your next workout.

After that comes the place where you take center stage: the training diary pages. These pages give you a place to make a workout plan that's customized for your level of fitness, your goals, and your schedule. You also have a place to record each workout and monitor your progress. Each spread is complete with a fitness factoid or a quote guaranteed to pique your curiosity.

The book closes with the Part of Tens, a couple of short chapters filled with a few more amusing tips. And finally, the index will help you locate anything you can't find on your own.

Icons Used in This Book

As with any *For Dummies* book, this one has icons to act as guideposts to special hints and notions along the way, each one offering a helpful perspective to consider as you plan your workout.

This icon highlights a quick hint that will help you train better and more efficiently.

Items flagged with this icon will help you to avoid accidents and injuries.

This icon is the graphic equivalent of a string tied around your finger, a reminder about something that you can't — or shouldn't — do without during your training or your race.

This icon flags training technique suggestions, workout gear recommendations, and fun facts you can use to amaze your friends at cocktail parties.

Information included with this icon offer suggestions that will make your workouts easier.

Where to Go from Here

The important thing about training is to get started *today.*
And start tracking your progress *today.* The sooner you start
to make use of this book's diary and log your workout
progress, the sooner you can see improvements in your daily
training regimen. So turn the page (or use the Table of
Contents or Index to get to the information you need the
most) and get going!

Part I
The Training Basics

In this part . . .

Ready to go? Good. But before you lace up your sneakers, pour yourself a cup of coffee, sit down, and spend a few minutes reading this section, where you'll learn how to get ready for a workout, train as efficiently as possible, and get ready for next time.

Chapter 1

Creating Your Workout Plan

*W*hat do you have in common with a world-class athlete and a James Bond supervillain? Each of you needs a plan. The good news is that you don't need to draw blood three times a day to check your lactate levels, and you don't need an evil laugh and a world map marking every missle silo to . . . *Ha Ha Hmmm . . . Rule the World!*

Even if you're not after a gold medal or global domination, but you simply want to lose a few pounds, a plan helps in any number of ways. It makes your workouts more efficient and helps you to see results more quickly.

Conversely, if you start a workout program without a plan, you're like that classic Sex Pistols song — don't know what you want, but you know how to get it.

Why Exercise Anyway?

Before you delve into the whats, wheres, and hows of creating your own exercise program, back up and think about *why* you exercise in the first place. You probably know a lot of the answers, but listing them may just be the difference between getting up for that 6:30 a.m. workout and hitting the snooze button.

- ✔ **You'll be healthier:** By exercising, you can reduce your risk of serious and even life-threatening diseases such as diabetes, heart disease, and cancer. There's even evidence that exercise can ward off the common cold.

- ✔ **You'll look better:** Exercising not only burns calories but also boosts your metabolism, which makes it easier to maintain your desired weight without resorting to the celery and ice cream diet.

- ✔ **You'll be less stressed:** Exercise produces endorphins — the same mood-altering brain chemicals that are targeted by everything from chocolate to illicit drugs. Runner's high is more than a myth.

- ✔ **You'll have fun:** Remember when you used to go out and play after school, running and jumping, riding and skating until you were exhausted? Well, pick the right exercise and that same kind of fun is still there for the taking.

Making Your Fitness Plan

If the road to fitness is a journey, then a fitness plan is your road map. You don't need to be a motivational guru to understand that before you can get in shape, you've got to identify some workout goals and figure out how to get from here to there.

First, you have to identify your destination, or your goal. In this section, I tell you how to do that. Once you know where you're going, it becomes a lot easier to map out the shortest route there, which I discuss later in this chapter.

Setting your fitness goals

In workouts and in life, goal setting can be both easy and hard. At its most basic level, setting a goal is as simple as identifying something you want. It can be as vague as, "I want to be happy." Or as specific as, "I want to be the executive vice president in charge of marketing by the end of September."

Workout-wise, you have the same range of choices. Your objective can be as general as wanting to be healthier and feel better and have some fun. Or it can be as specific as saying, "I want to break 50 minutes in the Independence Day 10K." Or, "I want to drop 12 pounds and two dress sizes so that I'm looking good for Chris's wedding in August."

The bottom line is that the quality of the goal you set is directly proportional to your chance of achieving it. If your goal is too vague, it can be almost impossible to measure your progress. ("Do I really feel healthier and feel better than I did last week?")

If the goal is too specific, that can be a problem too. If you become too goal-oriented — "I've been exercising for three weeks and my time (or waistline) hasn't come down at all" — it's easy to get discouraged by slow progress or minor setbacks.

The best goals are those that have both macro and micro components. Your macro goal might be, "I want to run the New York City Marathon next year." Your micro goal might be, "I want to run the 5K in town faster than I did last year." In short, your everyday goal should be an easily achievable, bite-size chunk of that larger goal. The short-term goal gives you a reason to work out today — "The 5K is ten days away" is a much better incentive for getting out of bed than, say, "The marathon is ten months away."

And once you achieve that micro goal, you can pat yourself on the back, because you did what you set out to do, and you also moved a little closer to your big objective, which makes it easier to set another micro goal.

Finding the time

The world's number-one all-purpose excuse? *I'm too busy.* Do you know anyone who's *not* too busy? I even hear it from my three-year-old son Ethan when I ask him to pick up his trains. "But, Daddy, I'm too busy." So let's find a way past the "B" word, shall we?

The first step is to make exercise a priority. Whether we write things down or not, every day each of us has a giant to-do list — with standing entries ranging from taking a shower to making enough money to pay the mortgage. So what you need to do is add one more thing that you absolutely, positively must do today: Get some exercise.

The best way to make sure that exercise becomes as automatic as brushing your teeth? Make it part of your schedule. Here are a few ways to incorporate exercise into your daily routine.

✔ **Do it early:** You remember Murphy's Law, right? Well, one of its axioms is that if you put off your workout until after work, and you go to the DMV, do grocery shopping, and drop the kids off at their friends' house, the following will happen. The DMV line will snake around the block, the baggers at the grocery store will stage a sit-down strike, and you'll get caught in a traffic jam on the way to the play date. In short, everything that can go wrong, will, and you'll be running an hour late, and today's workout will have to wait until tomorrow. If you work out first thing in the morning, you won't have to worry about life's little intrusions.

✔ **Multi-task:** Exercising can be tacked on to other chores, if you make it the first task, rather than the last. Stopping at the gym on your way to work, or right after you drop the kids off at school, is a great way to make sure that it gets done.

✔ **Get help:** Familes and friends can place demands on you that can keep you from exercising. Or they can help clear your schedule so that you have the time. If you're having trouble finding time to exercise, talk to the people in your life. Whether it's trading chores to get a big enough block of time to go to the gym, or just asking for a little good-natured nagging — "So, lard butt, have you gone running yet or what?" — your significant others can lend a hand in helping you get into shape.

More than the standard disclaimer

My lawyers want me to tell you that you should consult your physician before beginning a program of physical exercise. Okay, there I said it. But I'd like this to sink in more than the seat-belt demonstration on an airliner. After all, you wouldn't take a car that's been in storage for five years straight to the drag strip, now would you?

Well, if your car deserves a trip to the mechanic, don't you deserve a trip to your friendly neighborhood physician. A pre-exercise physical exam can uncover some underlying problems — anything from heart disease to a blood sugar imbalance — that could be exacerbated by exercise. So do the right thing — go see your doctor.

Setting Up Your Workout Schedule

Now that you've identified some goals and carved out some time to exercise, the next step is to make a workout plan. Some of the benefits of having a workout plan are obvious.

If you've made a plan in advance, it eliminates what coaches call "game-time decision-making." It allows you to glance at the day's schedule and go out and do it, rather than try to remember what your last workout was, and whether tomorrow's a rest day or not. Which means that you get out of the house and start breaking a sweat sooner.

But the biggest difference between having a workout plan and just going out and exercising is this: When you create a plan, you balance rest and recovery, and every workout has a specific purpose in helping you achieve your fitness goals. It's really about squeezing the maximum fitness benefit out of the minimum amount of time.

Build a smart plan and stick to it, and I guarantee you'll be stronger, fitter, and faster. And, if after a month or two you can suddenly fit into a pair of jeans that you thought were two sizes too small, well, so much the better.

The first thing you need to do is determine how many days a week you're going to work out. If you're just starting out, three is a good number. And it's best to balance workout days with rest and recovery days (see Chapter 4 for more about the importance of rest). For that reason, you might start out by working out on Monday, Wednesday, and Friday. Or Tuesday, Thursday, and Saturday if that suits you better.

And if you're doing cross-training — combining two or more activities in your workout plan — then it makes sense to alternate your activities in addition to your workouts. For example, if you're going to ride your bike twice a week, swim once a week, and do one weight training session, your schedule may shake out like the one in Table 1-1.

Table 1-1 A Typical Cross-Training Workout Schedule

Sun	Mon	Tue	Wed	Thu	Fri	Sat
Rest	30 min	Rest	30 min	Rest	40 min	Rest
	Bike		Swim +		Bike	
			Resistance training			

The specifics aren't as important as the general principles. In Table 1-1, I alternate the rest and exercise days. The two bike rides are separated by two and three days, respectively, to give you ample time to recover. The duration of the workouts increases gradually through the week. And since you're going to the health club to swim, that's a good day to put in a few minutes in the weight room.

Of course, you can feel free to modify this plan to fit your schedule, your level of fitness, and your goals.

What about next week? In general, it's good to keep your schedule pretty much the same from week to week. Schedule the longer workouts and gym sessions on the same day, if possible. And while you should add to the length of the workouts, as your fitness level allows, don't push it too hard. Adding more than 10 percent a week is only inviting injury.

Getting into Training

So you've already been doing this exercise thing for a while? Well, congratulations. Now may be the time for you to move from the land of the unstructured workout to full-fledged training.

Training? Don't get freaked out by the "T" word. Yeah, that's what athletes do, but in the end, your goals aren't really so much different from theirs. You want to get as fit as you can in as little time as possible, right? By focusing your training program, you can do just that.

Measuring your fitness

Every good fitness program needs three good measuring tools. You have one of the essentials right here in the form of this training diary. The other two you can buy at almost any sporting goods store — a watch with a stopwatch function and a heart-rate monitor. They form what a consultant might call a synergy.

- ✔ The watch tells you how long you worked out.
- ✔ The heart-rate monitor tells you how hard you worked.
- ✔ The training diary lets you keep track of your progress.

And all three together will motivate you to get out, identify your strengths and weaknesses, and help you get the most out of your training time.

While timing your workout is pretty basic, heart-rate monitoring was something that, until recently, only elite athletes did. At its most fundamental level, your heart rate is really the measuring stick of your cardiovascular fitness. If your speed goes up while your heart rate stays the same, then, congratulations, you're fitter. But even more importantly, your heart rate is the most reliable indicator of how your body is producing energy, which gives you the opportunity to target your training that much more accurately.

And while you can take your pulse by just putting a finger on an artery on your wrist or on your neck while you're exercising, it's far more convenient to just peek at your heart-rate monitor.

"But," you say, "I'm not an Olympic athlete." All the more reason why you need a heart-rate monitor. Olympic athletes actually have sort of a built-in heart-rate monitor, a sixth sense about how hard they're working, developed over years of training. They mostly use their heart-rate monitors to confirm what their bodies are already telling them.

Ironically, recreational athletes, who can benefit most from a heart-rate monitor, are the least likely to own one. Newbies are more likely to judge their workout by speed rather than real workload, so they're likely to overdo it if they encounter a hill, and loaf a little when they have a tail wind.

Do you fall into that camp? Try this test: During your next workout, guess your heart rate. If you're not consistently within ten beats, you need a heart-rate monitor.

Having trouble getting a reading from your heart-rate monitor early in your workout? Try licking the sensor. Most rely on the conductivity of your sweat to work properly, and saliva is the best substitute.

Maxing out — speaking from the heart

One bit of information that you need before you start a training program is your *maximum heart rate*. Throughout the rest of this chapter, different training intensities are expressed as a percentage of maximum heart rate. Here's the simplest way to determine your MHR:

- ✔ Women, subtract your age from 226. (A 33-year-old female would end up with a maximum heart rate of 193.)
- ✔ Men, subtract your age from 220. (A 33-year-old male calculates a maximum heart rate of 187.)

While this number should give you a reasonable ballpark rate, it doesn't take into account factors such as heredity and your present fitness level.

The other way of determining your maximum heart rate is by pushing yourself until you get there. The safest and most accurate way to do this is with a treadmill stress test administered by your doctor. And of course, before embarking on any exercise program, you should consult with your doctor.

The Building Blocks of Training

So what's the difference between a planned workout and just plain exercising? Well, in a planned workout, you build at least one of three things: strength, speed, or endurance.

These are the building blocks of all fitness — whether it's on a bike, a basketball court, or a skating rink. Every sport more strenuous than chess calls upon these three basic qualities in various proportions. But before I talk about how to build your fitness, I need to define the terms.

Endurance

Endurance is a pretty straightforward concept. It's the ability to run or ride or swim a little farther today than you did yesterday. Sure, some part of endurance is mental — it's a borderline obsessiveness that allows people to swim the English Channel or run an ultramarathon. But it's also physical attribute, the ability of your muscles and your connective tissues to keep going . . . and going . . . and going.

A buyer's guide to heart-rate monitors

A heart-rate monitor should have a readout that's big enough to read while you're exercising. The buttons should be big enough that you can manipulate them while you're on the go. The elastic chest strap, which actually takes the reading, should be comfortable both while you're at rest and while you're exercising. The most important function is the capability to set a target heart-rate range with an audible alarm that beeps when you're above or below it.

As for the more sophisticated programming options — anything from a post-workout readout of average heart rate to a full record of the workout that can be downloaded to your computer — let your love of gadgetry, or lack thereof, be your guide.

Failing to succeed

How hard should you be pushing yourself during a sprint? Harder. No, harder than that. No, even harder. Elite athletes do intervals until "failure." What does that mean exactly? It means that on your last set, you can barely stand up, or take one more stroke.

On a micro level, you have tried and you have failed. And on a macro level, you have most definitely succeeded.

And for endurance efforts, your body produces energy *aerobically* — taking in as much oxygen as it's consuming — and uses fat as its primary fuel.

Strength

Simply, strength is the ability to move mass, but it's more than just the ability to move a refrigerator or do 100 pushups. In most forms of exercise, whether it's swimming, running, or cycling, the mass that you're moving is, well, you. And improving your strength gives you the ability to move farther with every stride or stroke, as well as the ability to contend with natural obstacles such as head winds and hills.

For these kinds of high-power activities, your body often functions *anaerobically* — you're consuming more oxygen than you can take in — and uses carbohydrates for quick energy.

Speed

Speed is, you guessed it, the ability to move fast. And it's easy to measure, whether against a rival or against the clock. Simply, if you have any thoughts about competing, whether seriously or casually, you have the need for speed.

Speed workouts are usually highly anaerobic and use carbohydrate stores as a fuel source.

The Three Kinds of Workouts

Okay, so you understand what your goals are. Now how do you tailor an aerobic program to increase your abilities? Well for starters, your master plan should incorporate three different kinds of workouts, each addressing one of the three cornerstones discussed in the preceding section.

Long, steady distance

To improve your endurance, you're going to do *LSD* — long, steady distance — workouts. By building endurance, LSD workouts provide a base for your training schedule. They train your body to use fat as a fuel, which is the most efficient way to power your muscles for long-distance workouts. They also allow your body to recover from the stresses that your power- and speed-building workouts place on your body.

LSD workouts seem easy, and in a way, that's the problem. You feel like you should be doing more, and so you push yourself beyond the point at which you're getting the maximum training benefit. Discipline yourself to go slowly and keep your heart rate in the target range. Shoot for between 50 and 70 percent of your maximum heart rate on LSD workouts.

Strength training

While you can increase your strength by doing resistance workouts — running in sand, riding up hills, skating with really rusty bearings — the best way to get stronger is to hit the gym. A balanced whole-body program of weight lifting can increase your strength, help prevent injury, and even help you look better in a bathing suit.

It doesn't really matter whether you choose a machine-to-machine circuit or a series of light free-weight exercises. If you've never lifted weights before, ask a trainer at your gym or health club to show you proper form and help you design a workout plan. The key is stick-to-itiveness. It'll take about 12 to 16 weeks, working out two to three times a week, to really build your strength.

Unless your goal is to get pumped up Schwarzenegger-style, you should stay away from heavy weight/low rep exercises. Adding too much upper-body muscle could actually slow you down by adding a little power and a lot of extra weight.

Speed intervals

To get fast, you need to do sprint intervals. The idea is to run or pedal or swim as fast as you can for a short time — between 10 and 20 seconds. Then catch your breath and do it all over again.

In every muscle, there are fast-twitch and slow-twitch fibers. While an individual's proportion of fast-twitch to slow-twitch fibers is largely determined by genetics — Olympic sprinters got there by choosing their parents well — you can increase your percentage of fast-twitch fibers somewhat with speed training. Your heart rate should go completely into the anaerobic zone, the place where your body pulls out all its energy trump cards. This corresponds to a reading of between 85 and 100 percent of your maximum heart rate.

Building a Workout Plan

In order to maintain a consistent workout regimen, you need to get out your calendar. What follows is a 12-week training program, divided into three phases, that's guaranteed to get you in top shape in as little time as possible.

✔ Phase 1 of the program focuses on building an endurance base (see Table 1-2). You start out working out three days a week, all LSD workouts. By the end of this phase, you're exercising four days a week and are doing some strength workouts.

✔ Phase 2 of the program focuses on maintaining your endurance while building your power (see Table 1-3). You start out with one weight workout a week and increase it to two, while introducing some speed work by the end of phase two.

✔ Phase 3 of the program focuses on maintaining your strength and endurance, while adding some speed work (see Table 1-4).

Table 1-2 — Workout Plan: Phase 1

Week	Sun	Mon	Tue	Wed	Thu	Fri	Sat
1	45 min LSD	Rest	Rest	30 min LSD	Rest	Rest	20 min LSD
2	60 min LSD	Rest	Rest	30 min LSD	Rest	Rest	25 min LSD
3	60 min LSD	Rest	20 min LSD	Rest	30 min LSD	Rest	30 min LSD
4	75 min LSD	Rest	30 min Strength	Rest	30 min LSD	Rest	30 min LSD

Table 1-3 — Workout Plan: Phase 2

Week	Sun	Mon	Tue	Wed	Thu	Fri	Sat
5	75 min LSD	Rest	Rest	Strength	Rest	40 min LSD	Rest
6	90 min LSD	Rest	Rest	Strength	Rest	40 min LSD	Rest
7	100 min LSD	Rest	Strength	Rest	40 min LSD	Rest	30 min Strength
8	100 min LSD	Rest	30 min Speed	Rest	50 min LSD	Rest	Strength

Table 1-4			Workout Plan: Phase 3			
Week	**Sun**	**Mon**	**Tue**	**Wed**	**Thu**	**Fri**	**Sat**
9	30 min Strength	Rest	30 min Speed	Rest	40 min LSD	Rest	110 min LSD
10	40 min Strength	Rest	30 min Speed	Rest	40 min LSD	Rest	110 min LSD
11	40 min Strength	Rest	40 min Speed	Rest	50 min LSD	Rest	110 min LSD
12	50 min Strength	Rest	40 min Speed	Rest	50 min LSD	Rest	110 min LSD

What do you do when you reach week 12? Try the mainte-
nance week schedule in Table 1-5 for a few weeks, which
replaces one of the speed workouts with an LSD workout.

Table 1-5		Workout Plan: Maintenance				
Sun	**Mon**	**Tue**	**Wed**	**Thu**	**Fri**	**Sat**
90 min LSD	Rest	40 min Speed	Rest	50 min LSD	Rest	40 min Strength

No, the program isn't carved in stone, and you can feel free to
adapt this training plan to your schedule and your level of fitness. However, note that there are some overriding principles
in any good training program:

✔ You should alternate weight lifting or speed workouts
with LSD days or rest days to allow for recovery.

✔ Longer LSD workouts fall on a Saturday or a Sunday,
which gives you more flexibility in scheduling them.

✔ Your aerobic output will increase from week to week, by
no more than 25 percent a week during the endurance
phase and no more than 15 percent a week during the
power and speed phases.

Chapter 2

Just Warming Up

*A*lways be prepared. It's a good motto, even if you're not a Boy Scout. And prepared is exactly what you'll be, after reading this chapter. In these pages, you find out how to ensure that your workout will be, as the pharmaceutical companies say, safe, effective, and without unpleasant side effects.

In exercising, as in orienteering, a few minutes ahead of time spent getting yourself and your body prepared can pay big dividends down the road, making your workouts both more efficient and fun, as well as preventing injuries.

But unlike, say, getting your knot-tying merit badge, preparing properly for your workout is easy, if not always obvious. In this chapter, I discuss how to dress for comfort and efficiency, how to warm up and stretch effectively, and how to make the most of your workout time. So are you ready to get ready?

Bringing the Right Equipment

One of the nice things about exercising is that for the most part, it's gear free. But just because you can go out and exercise with just what you can carry in a gym bag, doesn't mean that the right equipment won't make your life a little easier. Here's how.

The right shoe on the right foot

A brief story about athletic shoes. A few years back, I went to my orthopedic surgeon with plantar fasciitis — an inflammation of a tendon that made it feel like someone was plunging an ice pick into the bottom of my feet. First off, he did what any doctor would do: prescribed some anti-inflammatories to alleviate the pain and told me to do some stretching exercises to keep the tendon flexible. Then he asked me a question. "What kind of shoes are you wearing?"

"Whatever's on sale," I responded.

He said, "With feet like yours, you should be wearing Brand X or Brand Y. Brand Z is pretty wide, like your foot, but they're not going to give you the support that you need."

I did the math. I had saved $10 on the last pair of running shoes I bought. And I was paying the doctor $200 for 15 minutes of his time.

So I went out and bought a pair of Brand X shoes. They fit great. More importantly, within a week, the plantar fasciitis was gone. And five years later, it's still gone. What more can you ask for?

 While I can't guarantee that picking the right footwear will keep the doctor away, I think there's a lesson here. Take some time to research the right footwear for your feet. Read magazine reviews. Check out the manufacturers' Web sites. Ask the advice of other athletes, and, yes, even your orthopedic surgeon. And once you find a brand and a model that works, stick with it. A shoe can't be a bargain if it comes complete with a trip to the doctor.

Getting a brand new bag

Do you have a gym bag? Great. Oh, you mean you don't? Then put down the book and go buy one, right now. Or soon anyway.

The right gym bag — and by that I mean one that's right for you — can make your life much easier. How? A sensible bag keeps your gear organized, which allows you to squeeze in a workout in a time slot where you once did nothing but scramble around looking for your tights and your lock.

What makes a good bag? One that's the right size — big enough to carry everything you need comfortably, but not so big that you're tempted to throw in the proverbial kitchen sink. Try to pick a style that you won't be ashamed to, say, carry to work.

The biggest practical need in a good bag is a way to segregate your wet clothes from your dry ones. The best bags have a partition, or a zippered compartment to keep the wet just-worked-out-in sweats away from the dry wearing-to-the-big-meeting clothes. Another big bonus is a breathable fabric — anything from Gore-Tex to mesh — which allows your workout gear to dry without getting moldy. And smellwise, a bag that breathes will make you and your friends breathe easier, too.

A Word about Workout Wear

Clothes may or may not make the man, but they *can* make your workout much more comfortable. And today's new generation of athletic wear is better than ever.

Indoor clothes

The all-cotton T-shirt has long been a staple of the athletic wardrobe. And there are good reasons for it. It's cheap. It's comfortable. And it's easy to launder. But the problem is that it also absorbs sweat like the proverbial mop, which can make it less than comfortable after half an hour of hard exercise.

For those reasons, you may want to consign those Gap T-shirts to your casual wardrobe and get something a little more sports specific for your workouts.

New polyester and polyester-blend fibers don't absorb sweat as readily as cottons and they wick moisture from the skin to the exterior to where it can evaporate. Pretty cool, eh? That's exactly what you'll be if you give these new school threads a try. Pretty dry, too. Athletic clothes that do the wicking routine usually have a hang tag explaining how the gee-whiz fabric works.

Why tights?

Sure, there's something sexy about skin tight fabric over a trim body, but don't assume that its form-fitting cut is just for show. Recent studies have shown that tights made of Lycra or some other highly stretchy material can actually help to prevent muscle pain.

Essentially, the fabric exerts a mild compression on your leg muscles, which reduces the vibration that can cause muscle fatigue, as well as minimizes any inflammation if you overdo it. In short, your tights are working the same way as a pair of support hose, or those burst-of-energy panty hose.

But don't overdo it. If your tights are too tight, they can constrict your circulation, and you could even injure yourself trying to wriggle inside. How tight is too tight? If it takes you longer to squirm into and out of your workout clothes than it does to actually work out, that's a hint that you need the next larger size.

Outdoor clothes

If you're working out outside, you have another set of obstacles to contend with — Mother Nature. And the problem, of course, is that the same clothing that keeps you warm can make you sweat enough that you get chilled anyway. But thanks in large part to man-made fibers, that has all changed. Here's what to look for:

- ✔ **High peformance polyester base layers** can wick moisture away from your skin so that the moisture evaporates before it makes you cold.

- ✔ **Fleece insulation layers** can keep you warm without bulk, and because they don't absorb moisture, they also won't get sweat-logged.

- ✔ **Breatheable outer layers,** like shell jackets or pullovers, can protect you from the wind and rain (but not the gloom of night). The real trick is that these advanced fabrics, coupled with venting systems such as underarm zippers, allow enough air circulation that you not only stay dry from the inside but also from the outside.

Warming Up to Warming Up

Do you have insurance on your house? On your car? Well, think of a good warm-up as insurance for your workout. Taking a few minutes before your workout to warm up can help prevent injuries and, yes, even boost your performance.

The pre-stretch warm-up

When I hurt my knee a few years back, I went to physical therapy to rehab it, and each session was like a gym workout on steroids — figuratively, of course. And the first thing my physical therapist did every session was put me on the stationary bike for about 15 minutes. Then, and only then, did we start a thorough and lengthy stretching routine before we hit the weights.

Why, I asked. First, my therapist replied, contrary to popular opinion, stretching doesn't really warm up your muscles. What it takes to increase the circulation to the muscles and the connective tissue is some light aerobic exercise.

Secondly, serious stretching is important, but it isn't risk free. Overly enthusiastic stretching of cold muscles and joints is almost as likely to *cause* an injury as it is to prevent one.

And after filing this advice away, I began to notice this pre-stretching warm-up as one of the biggest differences between professional athletes and the rest of us. Watch recreational athletes, and the first thing they do is get down and start to stretch. But watch pros prepare for a game, and you'll find that the team trainers make them begin their workouts with a brief round of aerobic exercise, and only after they've begun to work up a sweat do they begin to stretch.

Here are some activities you can try to get the blood circulating, literally:

- ✔ **Pedal a stationary bike:** It's an easy, low-impact workout that works your whole leg. Just remember to keep the RPMs high and the resistance very low.

- ✔ **Take a light jog:** Again, it's important to hold yourself back. You're not doing aerobic work, you're just trying to increase your heart rate.

A warm knee is a happy knee

Admit it. You like showing off your legs. Most athletes do. And while it does good things for your ego, it may not be doing good things for your joints.

Your knee, you see, is lubricated by something called synovial fluid. "If the knee joint gets cold, it makes the synovial fluid thicker," says a sports scientist with USA Cycling.

"Normally, it's the consistency of warm honey. When it gets cold out, it's like cold honey, and it doesn't work so well." How cold is cold? Well, most European coaches make their riders wear tights or leg warmers any time the temperature drops below 70°F. If you have chronic knee problems, you may just want to do the same.

> ✔ **Take a walk:** No, it's not sexy, but a brisk walk is a good way to get the old blood circulating. And if you're really resourceful, you can combine it with transportation, walking to the gym, or the beginning of your workout route.

If those ideas don't float your boat, just try something else to start the blood flowing. It doesn't really matter what you do as long as you keep the brakes on, so to speak, and don't go from breaking a sweat to working up a sweat.

Protecting your skin

When you're exercising outside, it's important to protect your skin. Some simple preventive measures can not only reduce the risk of premature aging but also serious, and increasingly common, problems such as skin cancer. The following are a few common-sense suggestions on ways to keep from tanning your hide:

> ✔ **Use sunscreen:** Your first line of defense is a sports-specific sunscreen that won't rub off when you sweat or sting if it drips into your eyes. And make sure the SPF is at least 30. Apply it on all exposed skin whenever you're exercising outside. And, yes, that means even on overcast days, when 70 percent of the sun's damaging rays still get through.

✔ **Cover up:** While it's smart to consider your clothes a first line of defense against the sun, understand that a lot of workout wear isn't very high on the SPF scale. A white cotton T-shirt gernerally comes in at an SPF of 10 or less. So if you're exercising on a day when the sun is intense, or in a sun-intense environment such as when you're running on the beach, it's smart to apply sunscreen underneath your clothes.

The Power of Stretching

For most of us, stretching has always been one of those things that you do because it's good for you — the athletic equivalent of eating your vegetables. And it's true that stretching prevents injury. But believe it or not, stretching can actually improve your performance, too.

Here's how it works. According to Dr. Vijay Vad, an orthopedic surgeon at New York's Hospital for Special Surgery, as you get older, the tendons that connect your muscles to your bones lose elasticity, kind of like a rubber band that's been left out in the sun too long. And as this happens, it restricts your ability to make the kind of explosive movements that you need to sprint or jump. (And, yes, this loss of the tensile properties in your tendons also makes you more susceptible to injury.)

The good news is that a program of slow, sustained stretching can actually restore much of the elasticity to your tendons, and in the process make you not only more limber, but more powerful, too. Here are a series of great upper- and lower-body stretches to get you started.

Lower body stretches

In most exercises your legs are in constant motion. A stretching routine can not only increase your range of motion, and reduce the risk of muscle pulls, but can also prevent or alleviate overuse injuries like tendinitis. Of course, you can feel free to supplement these stretches with your own favorites.

✔ **Quad stretch:** Standing upright, and holding onto something for balance if necessary, bring the heel of one foot up to your butt and grab your ankle with your hand. Gently pull the ankle up until you feel a stretch in your quadriceps (the muscles on the front of your thigh). Hold that position for 30 seconds and repeat with the other leg. (See Figure 2-1.)

✔ **Hamstring stretch:** While sitting on the ground, extend one leg in front of you and bend the other leg behind you, keeping the inside of your knee on the floor. Lean forward and grab the ankle of the extended leg. Don't curl your neck down, but try to move your chin toward your toes. You should feel a stretch in your hamstrings (the muscles on the backs of your thighs). Hold that position, without bouncing, for 30 seconds, and then repeat on the other leg.

Figure 2-1: The quad stretch.

✔ **A-stretch:** Stand with your feet spread about as far as they'll go. Slowly bend one knee until you feel a stretch on the inside of your non-bent leg. Hold for 30 seconds. Repeat with the other leg. (See Figure 2-2.)

✔ **Calf stretch:** Step forward with your right foot as if doing a lunge. Bend your forward knee (keep your back leg straight) until you feel a stretch in the opposite calf. Hold that position for 30 seconds and then stretch the opposite leg. (Using a wall or some other object to lean against, you can stretch both calves at once, as in Figure 2-3.)

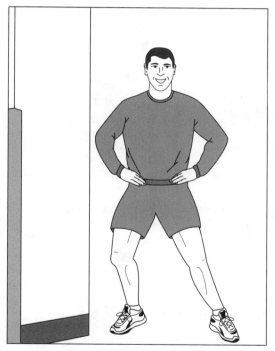

Figure 2-2: The A-stretch.

Figure 2-3: A double calf stretch.

> ✔ **Achilles stretch:** Stand with the balls of your feet on a step, but with your arches and heels dangling over. Hold onto a handrail for balance. Gently lower yourself until you feel a stretch in your Achilles tendons, just above the backs of your ankles. Hold that position for 30 seconds.

Upper body stretches

In most exercises, your upper body is especially subject to acute injury, from pulled muscles to more serious problems like ruptured discs and torn rotator cuffs. These stretches — along with any others you'd care to add — can help you reduce the risk of a trip to the doctor's office.

> ✔ **Hip stretch:** Lie flat on your back. Bend one leg up, grab your knee with both hands, and gently pull it toward your opposite shoulder. You should feel a stretch in your hips and buttocks. Hold the position for 30 seconds, again not bouncing. Repeat on the other leg.

Too sick to exercise? Maybe not . . .

You have a lousy head cold, and, well, you're just not feeling like yourself. Should you bag your workout? It depends. If you're running a fever, or if you have a hacking cough or significant chest congestion, you should wait until you get better. But if you have the common cold, or a touch of the flu, you don't necessarily have to stay in bed.

Research has shown that light to moderate exercise can actually boost your immune system and help you fight off whatever's bugging you. The key, of course, is to make the workout mellow — a light jog is fine, but running dozens of wind sprints will probably just make you sicker. Just as important, help your body regulate its temperature. If the thermometer is below freezing, consider running on the treadmill instead of around the park. And when you're done, get out of those wet clothes so that you don't get chilled, which, old wives' tales to the contrary, won't make you sick, but can make you more sick by reducing your body's ability to fight off germs and viruses.

✔ **Lower back stretch:** Lie flat on the floor, face down, with your legs straight and your arms extended. Pull your hands underneath you so that you raise your shoulders off the floor, but keep your hips on the ground. You should feel a stretch in your lower back. Hold for 30 seconds.

✔ **Upper back stretch:** Lie face-down with your legs extended and your hands next to your shoulders as if you were going to do a push up. Move your hips off the floor, while keeping your knees and shins on the ground. Then move your hips back until your arms are fully extended, and you feel a stretch in your upper back between your shoulder blades. Hold for 30 seconds.

✔ **Shoulder stretch:** While standing with your back straight, reach across your torso with your right hand and grasp your left upper arm. Allow the left arm to bend. Slowly, pull the left arm until you feel a gentle stretch in that shoulder. Hold for 30 seconds, then reach with your left hand across your body and grab your right upper arm. Pull and stretch.

✔ **Forearm stretch:** Hold your right arm straight in front of you, extending from the shoulder and keeping your elbow straight. Raise your hand at the wrist, until your fingers are pointing straight up. The position is as though you were giving someone a stop sign. Hold for 15 seconds. Lower your hand until your fingers are pointing straight down. Hold for 15 seconds, then repeat the stretch with your left arm.

No pain/no gain does not apply to stretching. Stretching shouldn't hurt. If you reach the point of pain, you may be injuring yourself, so back off a little.

Chapter 3

Conquering the Triathlon

- -

In This Chapter

▶ Swimming more smoothly

▶ Pedaling with aplomb

▶ Running with style

▶ Making faster transitions

- -

Triathlon. Even the word has a certain gravitas, conjuring up images of grimacing rail-thin runners, races that last all day and into the night, and a diet that consists of nothing but Gatorade and energy bars.

Well, it doesn't have to be that way. Think of this version instead. Hey, let's go for a swim in the lake. Wow, that was cool. What about riding bikes for a while? Excellent. And now that we're done pedaling, how about going for a run? Boy, I'm bushed. That's not the description of some kind of athletic death march, it's the outline for an almost-perfect summer vacation day back when you were nine years old, right?

If you slice up the task into bite-size bits, a triathlon can not only be manageable, it can be downright fun. And isn't that what it's supposed to be all about? (Although you can feel free to tell your thoroughly impressed friends and acquaintances what a test of fitness, courage, and yes, character the race is.)

In this chapter, I break down the triathlon to its component parts. You find out how to swim faster, both in the pool and in open water. You discover the tips of cycling fast and efficiently. I give you the skinny on how to bring it all back home in the running leg. And, of course, I throw in some tips for making lightning fast transitions. Ready? Set? Go!

Choosing Your Distance

Triathlons are like shorts. They come in different lengths. Here are the common distances for sanctioned races:

- ✔ **Sprint:** .5 mile swim/12 to 15 mile bike/5k (3.1 mile) run.

- ✔ **Olympic distance:** 1.5K (.93 mile) swim/40k (24.6 mile) bike/10K (6.2 mile) run.

- ✔ **Half Ironman:** 1.2 mile swim/56 mile bike/13.1 mile run.

- ✔ **Ironman:** 2.4 mile swim/112 mile bike/26.2 mile run.

Most beginners start with the sprint distance — only the fastest competitors actually sprint. If you have good open water swimming skills — most competitors find the swim leg the hardest — you could start at the Olympic distance. Ironman and half-Ironman distances take a major commitment of time and training.

In most triathlons, *drafting* — riding closely behind another rider who breaks the wind for you — in the bike leg is illegal, but in many Olympic distance events, drafting is legal. Which means that to be competitive, you need to be comfortable riding fast very close to other riders.

Improving Your Swimming

The bad news: Unlike a Labrador Retriever, you weren't born knowing how to swim. The good news: Neither were any of your competitors.

Swimming is by far the most technique intensive of the three triathlon disciplines. Which means that with a little attention to your stroke and your position in the water, you can shave seconds, and even minutes, off your time.

Streamlining in the water

Lesson one: Be like a fish. No, I don't mean lying on a bed of wilted greens between two lemon wedges. "Look at a fish and see how narrow they are," says Scott Rabalais, chairman of

U.S. Masters' Swimming Coaches Committee. "That's the way you want to be feeling when you're swimming."

Any trout can tell you that one of the keys to efficient swimming — going faster without expending more energy — is streamlining. Water offers much more resistance than air, so the less surface area you show in the direction you're swimming, the faster you'll go.

The first thing is to stay level in the water. Many swimmers don't balance well in the water, and drop their legs a foot or more below their torso, creating a lot of additional drag.

Once you've got the big body position licked, turn your attention to your extremities. Point your toes, point your fingers, and keep your arm as close to your head as possible when your hand enters the water.

Swimming slow to go fast

The reason why most swimmers go slowly? Because they swim too fast. Huh? "Some of the greatest swimmers in the world seem to have low turnover," says swim coach Scott Rabalais. "But they're holding on to the water very well." Translated that means although they may be taking fewer strokes than their competitors, these swimmers get more propulsion from each stroke.

Many recreational swimmers are notoriously inefficient taking as many as 20 more strokes per lap than more accomplished swimmers. The best way for recreational swimmers to gain speed is by emulating elite athletes: Take fewer strokes, but lengthen each stroke. Then count your strokes while you're training, and make a conscious effort to reduce your number of strokes per lap.

Swimming in open water

Swimming in a pool is one thing, but swimming in open water is quite another; the lack of chlorine is the least of your challenges. Even if you're a budding Ian Thorpe in the health club pool, you'll have a few adjustments to make once you start swimming al fresco. Here are some tips to help you make the transition.

Staying straight: navigating in open water

No matter where your next triathlon is held, here are two guarantees: there won't be any lane ropes and there won't be a stripe painted on the bottom of the river, lake, or bay. While it's easy — perhaps even inevitable — to stay straight and on course when you're swimming laps at the YMCA, it's a very different matter in open water.

 To get your bearings, focus on a distant object — anything from a turn buoy to something on the shoreline. Then at some predetermined stroke interval — every 20 strokes in calm water, every 5 if there's a heavy current — lift your head out of the water and make sure that you're still on course.

The advantage of swimming straight — aside from avoiding the whole swept-out-to-sea scenario — is that you'll cover less total distance, and eliminate those time- and energy-sapping course corrections.

Doing the wave: negotiating choppy water

A modern pool does a remarkable job of killing waves that affect even the smallest body of water. But even a lake has swells and currents, and larger bodies of water can get down-right rough.

 The biggest technique adjustment is to make your recovery — the part of the stroke where your arms are out of the water — much higher. If you don't, you're likely to spend much of the stroke with your arms completely underwater. Not much fun. So get your arm out of the water and high in the air quickly, and back in the water just as quickly. The less time your hand spends at the water surface, the less likely it will be affected by waves and chop.

The other tactic for dealing with waves and swells is to get used to swimming underwater for a few strokes. That way if you see you're likely to get buffeted by a particularly large wave, you can glide under it smoothly and efficiently rather than bodysurfing over it.

Chilling out: cold water concerns

Dealing with cold water is largely an equipment issue. Wearing a wetsuit is a must in colder races, and longer wet-suit that reaches to your ankles and wrists pays an added dividend when the temperature really plummets. In warmer water, you should slather up with Vaseline, which acts as insulation. And in any case, a swim cap can help reduce heat loss from your head.

The cold can also affect your breathing. Many swimmers find that they subconsciously hold their breath when the water's very cold. This doesn't make your breathing any easier. So even when it's so chilly that you'd swear you'd be blowing ice cubes, keep those bubbles coming.

Making contact: swimming in a crowd

While pool swimming isn't a contact sport, swimming in a triathlon is a different matter entirely. Several hundred triathletes gathered at the starting line will all be competing for the same stretch of water at the beginning of the swim leg. For the first few minutes, you'll just have to accept a little jostling, and hope that no one kicks you in the face. But as the field strings out a little, you can usually find some clear water by moving toward the outside of the *turn buoys* that mark the course.

Swimmer traffic isn't always negative. You can often save some precious time and energy by drafting another swimmer (swimming in his or her wake).

Staying Safe in Open Water

You can open the newspaper every morning for years, and never hear about someone drowning in their local health club lap pool. But every couple of weeks during the swim season, you'll hear about someone who drowned — or disappeared — in a lake, river, or ocean. This isn't meant to scare you, just make you think about safety. Here are some simple rules:

 ✔ **Know your limitations:** Before you tackle a triathlon or an open-water swim, be realistic about your swimming abilities. If you hang on to the edge of the pool for a second at the end of every lap to help you catch your breath, or grab the lane rope when you swallow a mouthful of water or get a cramp, think about what you'll do when you're in the middle of a lake, a bay, or the ocean. Obviously, the place to practice open-water skills is in a pool.

Keeping your goggles from fogging

It's hard to swim when you can't see. So, how do you keep your goggles from fogging up? The simplest solution — if not the most sanitary — is to lick the inside of your lens with saliva and don't wipe it afterward.

You can also try an anti-fog solution made by a goggle manufacturer. Some particularly fog-prone triathletes actually leave a few drips of water sloshing around inside their lenses to help keep them clear.

✔ **Don't swim alone:** While you'll have plenty of company when you're racing, training is a different story. So if you're going for an open-water swim, recruit a friend to swim along. If either of you needs help, this buddy system will prove invaluable, because your partner will be able to help you a lot sooner than a lifeguard, or vice versa. If either or both of you has taken a lifeguarding course, so much the better.

✔ **Check with the guards:** If you're swimming in a guarded area, it's a good idea to talk to the lifeguards before you head out for a long swim. First, they won't start blowing their whistles once you get more than 25 yards from shore, which is where you can get in some valuable training without having to look out for casual swimmers in too-tiny tankinis. And they'll keep an eye on you, which could literally be a lifesaver, if you need help.

✔ **Be visible:** Whatever your swim ensemble, add a brightly colored swim cap to it. This not only makes it easier for passing watercraft to avoid you, it also can help a lifeguard or rescue worker spot you in the event of an emergency.

The Swim-to-Bike Transition

Want to improve your time without so much as a single extra stroke, pedal, or stride? Work on your transitions. Fumbling with your wetsuit or your shoes for 30 seconds can cost you as much as a quarter mile on the road. So here are some tips for making a smooth transition from the swim leg to the bike.

✔ **Shed your wetsuit:** A wetsuit can speed up your swim leg, but you could waste almost all of that edge in taking it off. Applying Vaseline to your wrists and ankles can help it slip off all in one motion. You can also get a bit of an edge by shedding your suit at the water's edge — and handing it to a waiting friend — which will enable you to run much faster and more comfortably to your bike. And if you have to wear a singlet for the bike leg, you can save precious moments by wearing it underneath your wetsuit.

✔ **Spot your bike:** Ever lose your car in a shopping mall parking lot? Then why do you think you won't do the same with your bike in a crowded transition area. Mark your bike with something bright — anything from a beach towel draped over your handlebars to a neon flag on a fiberglass pole clamped to the rack — and use that marker to zero in on your mount. But this is no substitute for knowing the lay of the land — doing a dry run from the water's edge and then counting the rows to your bike.

✔ **Point it down the road:** When you're racking your bike, make sure the front wheel is pointing out. Turning the bike wastes valuable seconds.

✔ **Arrange your stuff:** Place a towel in front of your bike, so that you can wipe the sand off your feet. Put your helmet upside down on the handlebars, with your sunglasses inside.

✔ **Clip your shoes to your bike . . . or not:** Virtually all elite triathletes will leave their shoes clipped to their pedals, get on the bike barefoot, pedal a few strokes and then put their feet into their shoes. Should you do this? It depends. This is an advanced move that will only save you a few seconds at best, and if you fall or have to stop to adjust a shoe, you'll lose all of that edge and lots more. Some competitors even suggest that putting on their shoes before they get on the bike saves them time because they get up to speed faster.

✔ **Practice, practice, practice:** The real key is to practice your transitions, over and over again. Try to reproduce potential race conditions. Take a cold shower, and then try to shed your wet wetsuit, dry off, put on your helmet, and get right on the bike. These drills will not only increase the likelihood of a smooth transition, they'll also prevent a small mistake, like dropping your helmet, from becoming a full-fledged disaster.

The Bike Leg

Pedaling is actually a pretty basic skill — just watch a three-year-old on a Big Wheel. But pedaling properly? Well, that's an art. A proper pedal stroke — unlike a grown-up version of Big Wheel pedal-mashing — asks your feet to perform a complex, counterintuitive task, and do it precisely, thousands of times in an hour of riding, all while your conscious brain is occupied with small matters, like staying psyched for the run still to come.

As with most complex skills, pedaling can be broken down into simple steps. Here are the three secrets of pedaling properly: positioning your foot, choosing the right gear, and pedaling in circles.

Positioning your foot

The pedals on your bike have an axle that attaches to the crankarm. Your mission, and no, you can't choose not to accept it, is to put the ball of your foot on that axle, and keep it there while you're pedaling. And I mean the ball of your foot, not your arch and not the front of your heel. It's possible to pedal a bike while using the pedal as an arch support, but not very well, and definitely not without looking like a geek.

That's why most serious riders use toe clips or cycling shoes and clipless pedals. And if you're going to spend any time in the saddle, you've got to get this ball-over-the-axle position exactly right, because efficient and injury-free cycling begins with a good foot position.

It's also important to keep your foot straight while you're pedaling — not pigeon-toed or duck-footed. How can you tell if your foot's straight? If you look down and see that your thigh is parallel to the top tube of the bike, your foot position is probably pretty good.

As for the vertical relationship between your foot and the pedal, just go with the flow. If you just pedal naturally, at the top of the pedal stroke (12 o'clock) your toes are about even with your heel, while at the bottom of the stroke (6 o'clock) you're likely be on your tiptoes a little, with your heel above your toes. Keeping a loose ankle joint to allow for this subtle movement makes for a smoother pedal stroke, but the active "ankling" motion that some cycling books advocate is really overkill and will likely leave you with nothing more than sore ankles.

Choosing the right gear

The second step to righteous pedaling is choosing the right gear. Many novice triathletes choose too high a gear, figuring they'll go faster that way. Nope, it doesn't work that way, any more than you can win a tollbooth drag race by starting your Chevette off in fourth gear.

The problem with pushing a higher gear is that you also pedal slower. If riding feels like you've been doing squats for an hour, then you're riding in too high a gear. Pedaling in too high a gear is also one of the quickest ways to sore knees. And the lactic acid that builds up from pushing too high a gear will not only affect your bike leg but also make your legs feel like lead through the run leg.

The key to riding efficiently is to keep your pedal cadence high — scientific studies suggest that cyclists pedal most efficiently at between 80 and 100 revolutions per minute (RPM).

How do you know how fast you're pedaling? Well, you could just get your watch and count. But that's kind of a drag. You could buy a cycle computer with a cadence function. Not a bad idea if you want one anyway. But you can get the same information for free at your health club. Most stationary exercise bikes have a cadence (or RPM) readout. Pay attention to this readout the next time you're there. If you're trudging away at 70 RPM, then lower the resistance until you get to that magic 90 RPM mark. Try to stay in that range during your next few workouts — keeping that pace will soon become second nature.

Now, take that lesson on the road. On a flat stretch of road, use your muscle memory to get to that magic 90 RPM mark. If you err, err on the side of pedaling too fast. If you find it too hard to pedal, then shift to a lower gear — go to a larger cog on your freewheel. If you feel like a mouse in a Habitrail, scurrying furiously but getting nowhere fast, then shift to a higher gear/smaller cog. The idea is to find a gear that lets you feel some resistance, but not too much.

Pedaling in circles

Take a close look at the chainring attached to your bicycle's pedals. What is it shaped like? A banana cream pie? A smiley face? A PJ Harvey CD? No, this isn't a Rorschach test. Whatever you think it looks like, it's round.

And doesn't it follow, therefore, that your pedal stroke should be round, too? That's why top triathletes use a high speed, super-round pedal stroke. It's called *spinning*.

For the moment, think about your chain ring as a clock face. Most people pedal a bike a little like they walk — push down with one foot, and then push down with the other. In short, they're doing almost all of their pedaling between two o'clock and four o'clock. That's called *pedaling squares,* and it's all right for the bike path, but there is a better way for the competitive rider.

The key to more efficient pedaling is to use more of the clock. When your foot crosses the 12 o'clock point, consciously think about pushing the pedal forward, as well as down. The downstroke between two and four o'clock more or less takes care of itself.

When your foot reaches four o'clock, shift your focus and think about pulling back, as if you were scraping something off the bottom of your shoe. And if it helps you, you can even think about pulling up with your back foot as the pedal comes around — between say eight o'clock and eleven o'clock.

Getting aero

It's a fact. Your biggest foe on the bike leg of a triathlon is the wind. Most of your effort goes toward moving your bike and your body against air resistance. Bike racers combat this by drafting with their fellow racers, but in most triathlons, this practice is illegal.

And while expensive carbon fiber-bladed wheels and other aerodynamic doodads can help you cheat the wind, your biggest asset is an efficient position.

The idea is to minimize your frontal area as much as possible, keeping your head down, your back flat, and your hands in front — a position known as the *tuck*. This kind of sleek riding style doesn't happen overnight, so when you're training, you should be not only aiming to get stronger but also practicing staying low and compact on the bike.

The aero bars used by most triathletes can make it difficult to turn, and often keep the brake levers out of the rider's reach. That's why these bars are illegal in most bicycle road races. So when you're training, only assume your tuck on flat, straight, lightly trafficked roads.

Maximizing your turns

While most triathlons are relatively straight and flat, a brief primer on turning can keep you from losing time on the twisty bits. Good turning technique requires more than a little body English. You want to lean your body to the inside of the turn while turning the handlebars only gently. Centrifugal force takes care of a lot of this for you — you're probably leaning the bike a little without even realizing it.

But truly effective cornering entails giving Mr. Newton's forces a hand. The first thing you have to do is stop pedaling and move your inside pedal — the pedal leaning into the turn — to the 12 o'clock position and the outside pedal to 6 o'clock so that you don't scrape your inside pedal on the ground. Some coaches also suggest pointing your inside knee toward the ground — but you have to realize that the knee move isn't as important as the adjustment you have to make at your hips to make it happen. Ideally, you want to lean into the turn with your hips while keeping your shoulders relatively level to the ground.

Laying bricks

A *brick* is a double workout that sim- race conditions. Start with a medium-
ulates the second transition, getting long ride, and go straight into a race-
off the bike and making the transition pace run. The key is a quick transition
to a race-pace run with lactic-acid from the bike to the run — just as if
laden legs. These workouts are hard, you were in a race.
but vital to getting your body used to

The other part of the turn business is tactical. Your goal is to
take the shortest, straightest line through a turn. The bike
wants to go in a straight line. So you want to find the line that
lets the bike do what comes naturally. Start at the far end of a
turn, go straight across the *apex* — the inside point of the
turn — and end up on the far side of the road, the way a race
driver might.

The Bike-to-Run Transition

The bike-to-run transition isn't quite as complicated as the
first transition, but there are a few ways you can gain a few
seconds.

- ✔ **Gear down:** In the last few miles of the bike leg, shift to
  a lower gear and spin hard. The lower gear will help you
  negotiate the traffic in the transition area, as well as
  helping to flush the lactic acid out of your legs so that
  you'll be able to start faster in the run leg.

- ✔ **Be organized:** Lay a towel down on the ground, with
  your singlet below it — remember to pin on your
  number — and your shoes on top.

- ✔ **Don't shortchange your shoes:** Sure, it's great to save a
  few seconds with elastic laces or lace locks. But don't
  shortchange your fit. If your insole is wrinkled or your
  feet are too wet, you're risking a blister that could cost
  you in both time and discomfort.

Running on Empty

The good news is that you're heading for home. The bad news is that your body, which has gutted out the swim and the bike, wishes you were home already. Here are some ways to make the run leg less like a death march and more like a victory lap.

Building an efficient stride

The Road Runner was right. The most efficient way to run is to take lots of fast little strides and not just lope along Wile E. Coyote-style. Sports scientists suggest by keeping your feet close to the ground and moving forward instead of up, you can shave precious seconds off your race times. To tack another half mile onto your morning runs, you can shorten your strides — even by a few inches — and up your RPMs.

Most recreational runners average about 80 strides per minute, while top middle distance runners have stride rates of over 100.

One of the best places to practice adjusting your strides is on a treadmill, where you can look at your watch and count your strides without having to worry about cars, curious dogs, or uneven pavement.

Knowing your race strategy

No, it's not exactly mapping out a zone defense in football, but running a good triathlon does entail some strategy and preparation, both mental and physical. Here are some hints to help you run your best time.

> ✔ **Have a plan:** As Elaine said to Benjamin in *The Graduate*, "I don't want you to go . . . until you have a plan." Before you head to the starting line you should have a target time. But make sure that it's realistic. Trying to run 30 seconds faster than your best 5K? That's realistic. Trying to break 20 minutes when you've never broken 25? Fuggedaboudit.

✔ **Start slowly:** It's really easy to get caught up in the excitement of the moment and go out too fast. Going anaerobic in the first half mile is a recipe for disaster. So consciously slow your pace over the first mile, and check your time at the first distance marker so that you can make sure you're running as slowly as you think you are.

✔ **Don't forget to hydrate:** Make sure that you plan for water stops during the run leg. It's especially important to drink early, chugging some water before you're thirsty. In longer races — Olympic distance and up — make sure to consume a few calories on the road as well.

✔ **Sticking to your pace:** First off, before you start you should know what mile splits you have to hit in order to achieve your target time. Believe me, it's tough doing division in your head while you're running. And once you settle into your race groove, try not to get distracted by subjective factors — how you feel or the pace of your fellow runners. Your stopwatch and your heart-rate monitor are much more objective judges of whether you should speed up or slow down.

✔ **Finish strong:** Sure you're tired. But you'll have plenty of time to rest after you cross the finish line. So over the race's last mile, pick up the pace. And when the finish line is in sight, that's the time for a full-on sprint. You might catch a couple of fading front-runners, shave a few seconds off your time, and give you the satisfaction that you gave all you had to give.

The Mental Side of Racing

If you're running as hard as you should be, you'll probably have some moments during the race when you're feeling pretty bad. This is when your mental resolve comes into play. Follow these guidelines and you'll be able to finish strong no matter how much you're suffering.

✔ **Think positively:** Is the race half over, or do you still have half the race to run? The most successful runners are optimists, able to put a positive spin even on a tough situation.

✔ **Remember the Alamo:** As Nietzsche said, "That which does not kill you makes you strong." So when you're facing a crisis, marshal your resources by remembering your toughest races and how you plowed through those few rough patches to finish strong.

✔ **Be your own drill sergeant:** Sometimes a tough love approach is what you need. Remind yourself about how hard you trained, and if you even think about dropping out, soldier, you're going to put yourself on KP duty so fast your head'll spin, got it?

✔ **Distract yourself:** It's really easy to get wrapped up in how bad you feel. So just try and dissociate yourself from your suffering. Hum a song. Try and remember lines from *The Godfather, Part II.* Look around for attractive runners of the gender of your choice. Think about anything but your labored breathing.

✔ **Make micro goals:** Don't think about the fact that you're four miles from the finish. Instead, say to yourself, I'm going to run hard until I get to the firehouse a quarter mile down the road. And when you reach the firehouse, find a new, easily achievable target.

Chapter 4

Cooling Down and Fueling Up

*T*o paraphrase the novelist Dorothy Parker, I hate exercising, but I love having exercised. Okay, that's not quite true. While the act of exercising often involves significant discomfort, there are few things in this world that compare with the afterglow of having just completed a great workout.

But while it's tempting to kick back as soon as you're done sweating, resist the temptation. The truth is, the minute your last workout is over, the preparation for your next workout is beginning.

The good news is that a lot of that preparation is fun — it involves high-on-the-hit-parade activities like eating, drinking, resting, and gloating over your accomplishments.

In this chapter, I discuss how to cool down, eat right, replenish your fluids, and rest the right way.

The Cool-Down

Did you ever watch the Kentucky Derby? Do the horses slam on the brakes as soon as they cross the finish line? Of course not. Well, you shouldn't either. After your workout, you need a few minutes to allow your body to make a smooth and gradual transition from exercise to rest.

You need to give your heart rate an opportunity to slow from its exercise-induced frenzy to a calmer, resting rate. A cool-down also gives your muscles the opportunity to flush out the lactic acid — the by-product of anaerobic exercise that's commonly known as liquid pain — that would otherwise make you oh-so-sore the next morning.

So how do you achieve this graceful progression from the sweating state to the post-sweating state? Simple. Just slow down. If you're doing an aerobic exercise, simply taper down your speed and resistance. If you're running, slow to a jog, and then to a walk. If you're swimming, slow down your stroke. If you're on a bicycle, shift down a gear or two and gradually pedal more slowly. Most exercise machines that you find in the gym — stair climbers, elliptical trainers, and stationary bikes — do this for you by building in a cool-down period at the end of each pre-programmed workout.

As a rule of thumb, five minutes is a good length of time for a cool-down, which is why most machines have this length of time pre-programmed. But listen to your body, too, and feel free to extend your cool-down time after a particularly intense workout session.

The morning after

Do you ever feel the peak of your soreness two days after a workout? There's a good reason for this. While the muscle pain you feel the day after exercise is largely caused by the aforementioned lactic acid buildup, the soreness you feel a couple of days later is caused by microtears in your muscles being repaired.

In moderate amounts, this pain is your body telling you that it's getting stronger. If you're experiencing so much pain that it's affecting your next workout, then it should be a signal for you to cut back. That old saying, "no pain, no gain," is right, but only to a point.

If you're doing resistance training, just shift to aerobic mode for a few minutes and jog, walk, or pedal for a few minutes to get your body in motion. A round of light post-workout stretching can also help your form.

Resting to Get Stronger

Here's the news you've been waiting for. If you want to get fitter, it's just as important to rest well as it is to work out hard. Elite athletes know this. They understand that while they're resting, their bodies are recovering from the day's exertion. "Recovery is just as important as the workout," says Steve Johnson, an exercise physiologist with USA Cycling. "The purpose of the workout is to stress the body and let it repair itself. The benefit of the workout only happens after you've recovered."

That's why it can be smart to make a workout plan that allows for a couple of non-consecutive days off during the week, especially after a particularly hard workout, and to restrict yourself to "active rest."

What's active rest? It's not vegging out on the couch or surfing the Web. It's moderate activity of the kind that you'd do to warm up for or cool down from a workout:

✔ Do some gentle stretching.

✔ Take a walk.

✔ Shoot a few baskets.

✔ Mow the lawn.

Active rest is anything that gets you moving without really breaking a sweat. This keeps your muscles from getting stiff and helps get the blood circulating to the connective tissue in your hips, your knees, and your ankles. And as long as you take it easy, your body will be able to divert its energy reserves into helping repair the damage that yesterday's intense workout inflicted, and it will build stronger muscles in the process.

Refueling Your Body

You know the old saying, "You are what you eat." So do you really want to be a Big Mac, a large order of fries, and a chocolate shake the next time you hit the gym? When you're exercising, food isn't food, it's fuel. Which is why you need to think before you chew.

Eating before your workout

This is a balancing act. You need to eat enough to give you enough energy for your workout, but not so much that you end up slowing yourself down. In practical terms, proper pre-exercise fueling is mostly a matter of monitoring not only *how much* you eat, but *what* you eat.

As you found out after you left the all-you-can-eat buffet at Enchilada World, some foods are more easily digested than others. Generally, this means focusing on easily-digested car-bohydrates and keeping fats to a minimum. If you're working out in the morning, cereal or yogurt is a better bet than a triple cheese omelet with a side of sausage. (I found this one out the hard way on a particularly strenuous bicycle ride following a particularly indulgent brunch.) For lunch, smart fueling means bypassing the bacon double cheeseburger with a crème brulee chaser and going for the pasta salad with the dressing on the side.

Why are foods that are okay when you're chilling out such a no-no when you're exercising? Chalk it up to evolution. Back in the days when your ancestors were being chased by saber-toothed tigers, they needed all the help they could get. So your body developed a response to this fight-or-flight situation. When you're running away from a woolly mammoth — or just pedaling up a big hill — your body funnels most of its resources to your muscles, postponing non-essential functions, like digestion. So eating easily digestible foods allows you to keep your muscles well fueled and keeps your stomach from rebelling. In short, you could say that it's about staying on the right side of the line between eating and being eaten.

Eating during your workout

Should you eat during your workout? Probably not. If you're just going to the gym or for a short run, you can wait until you get home. But if you're running a half-marathon, or going on a 50-mile bike ride, you should plan for some on-the-go refueling. The key is to do it early, before your energy reserves run low, and in small amounts and in regular intervals so that it's easily digested.

No, I don't mean you should stop at the drive-through window. A couple of bites of an energy bar or a little bit of fruit is enough. And keep in mind, I'm defining eating in the broadest possible way — that is, taking in calories. So if you chug some fruit juice or a sports drink, as far as your body's concerned, that's eating.

What should you eat? From a nutritional standpoint, it should be mostly carbohydrates, with a little bit of fat to mellow out the blood-sugar spike that can come from too much sugar. There is a multi-million dollar industry trying to get you to choose energy bars and energy gels for your in-ride nutritional needs. They're generally easy to eat, and nutritionally, they've done most of the thinking for you. If you like the way they taste and they make you feel more like a triathlete, go right ahead. But they're not magic. You probably have some perfectly good energy foods in your kitchen cupboard, such as those in Table 4-1.

Table 4-1	Food for Exercise			
Food	*Calories*	*Carbohydrates*	*Fat*	*Protein*
4 fig bars	200	46 g	0 g	2 g
3 Rice Krispie treats	225	45 g	4.5g	1.5 g
1 Milky Way Lite bar	170	34 g	5 g	1 g
1 Power Bar	225	42 g	2.5 g	10 g
2 Bananas	220	58 g	0 g	2 g

The bonk

Are you one of those people who hates to stop at a gas station? You'll run your car until it's almost at E, right at E, and even a little bit below E. Did you ever push it too far? Well, when your body runs out of fuel during the middle of a long workout — more than an hour — it's called *the bonk.* While it sounds kind of fun, the symptoms aren't: sudden, extreme weakness, often accompanied by lightheadedness, nausea, and/or severe hunger.

Fortunately, it only happens during endurance events — triathlons, 100-mile bike rides, and marathon runs — and the prevention is simple: Eat before you exercise. Eat small amounts frequently while you're on the road. And don't wait until you feel hungry. By then, it's probably too late.

A linguistic note: In French, the bonk is called *la fringale,* a word so euphonic that a fine French restaurant in San Francisco adopted it as its name. Funny how the French can make something so unpleasant sound romantic.

As you can see, there's not all that much difference between performance food and what your mother would dismiss as junk food. All have a good amount of carbohydrates and an acceptably low level of fat, and they can be eaten easily while you're running or riding. And if you stop to eat, your choices widen even further.

Eating after your workout

As soon as you're done with your workout, head for the cupboard, and get some carbohydrates into your system. Energy bars or drinks, fruit, pretzels, just about anything will do. It's not the time for a full meal, but an important chance to replenish your energy reserves.

And the timing is important. For the first half-hour after your workout, your body is primed to replace the carbohydrates you used to power your muscles during your workout. Once that window of opportunity has passed, you simply can't top off your tank as effectively.

After a couple of hours, it's time for a full meal. Here's the time for that well-balanced diet with an eye toward your long-term energy needs. It's a good time to fuel up with protein — something lean, like a chicken breast, pork tenderloin, or piece of fish. Some veggies add fiber and all sorts of nutrients to the mix. Round out the meal with a small side of complex carbohydrates — a baked potato, a portion of pasta, or even just some bread. As for the fats, just keep it in perspective. In moderation, fats are a necessary part of a balanced diet. What that means is that while an occasional pat of butter or sprinkle of grated cheese won't hurt you, you should pass on the ribeye steak.

The Hydration Quotient

Do you ever get home from a workout, and before you step into the shower, you step on the scale? "Three pounds lighter than this morning," you congratulate yourself. While it's certainly gratifying to watch those numbers go down, the reality is that you're probably a little less fat and a whole lot dehydrated.

There are a lot of reasons why water is the most important nutrient there is. Water — in the form of sweat — helps your body regulate its core temperature, and if you don't replenish your body's supply, it's like running your car with the radiator only half full. When you mix dehydration with exertion, the result can be heat exhaustion and even, rarely, heat stroke. In its more moderate forms, dehydration can cause muscle cramping and even make you more susceptible to muscle pulls.

So drink. Lots. In the hours before your workout, remember to drink a couple of nice large glasses of water. As long as you're sticking to water, it's almost impossible to drink to excess.

Drinking while you exercise is almost a Zen thing. You need to drink before you're thirsty. If you wait until you're thirsty, you're already dehydrated, and you're fighting a losing battle. Plan to drink at least four ounces every 15 minutes — more often if it's really hot — and you'll be fine.

And don't stop rehydrating after you exercise. In the hours after a workout, you still need to drink to rehydrate your body. It's also important to throw some electrolytes into the mix. Energy drinks help your body replenish these vital chemicals, but sensible eating — pretzels for sodium, a banana for potassium — can also do the job.

How can you tell if you're dehydrated? Well, if I may be so crude, simply look at the color of your urine. If it's clear, or almost clear, you're well hydrated. If it's dark yellow, hit the water fountain, now.

Are You Overtraining?

There is such a thing as too much of a good thing. If you don't believe me, ask the third runner-up in a hot dog eating contest. The same goes for fitness. There's a fine line between building up and tearing down, and it's easy to veer onto the wrong side of it. How do you know if you're training too hard? Listen to your body. Do you feel chronically tired? Like you're constantly on the verge of getting sick? Are you having trouble sleeping?

Those admittedly vague symptoms can all be symptoms of overtraining, especially if you've increased the duration or intensity of your workouts in the past week or two. The best objective way to monitor your training is to check your resting heart rate before you get out of bed in the morning. If your exercise program is working, your resting heart rate should stay basically the same or even gradually drift slightly downward as your fitness increases. If you find that your resting heart rate is increasing, it's a sure sign that your body's under stress.

Fortunately, unlike the common cold, there's a cure for overtraining. Just take a day or two off, and when you go back to training, take it a little easier until your first-thing-in-the morning heart rate settles back down.

Dealing with Injuries

Injuries are a part of athletics. Despite all your careful preparation, eventually you'll suffer some kind of an injury. The key of course is to treat the injury aggressively so that you can return to action as soon as possible.

Acute injuries

Ouch! That's the sign of of an acute injury. One minute you're exercising and the next minute you're writhing in pain.

If you're experiencing severe pain, numbness, or restricted movement in a joint after a fall, see your doctor immediately to rule out a broken bone or a serious dislocation of the joint.

For less serious orthopedic injuries — such as mild sprains or bruises — follow the RICE regimen (**R**est, **I**ce, **C**ompression, **E**levation) outlined later in this chapter, and if the injury doesn't heal within a reasonable period of time, see your doctor anyway.

Overuse injuries

Overuse injuries, on the other hand, tend to sneak up on you. You're a little sore one day, a little better the next, a little more sore the day after that. And then one day you wake up and you can't walk down the stairs.

To prevent overuse injuries, be smart and listen to your body. If you're training for an event, increase your workload gradually. If you're experiencing pain during or after exercise, take a few days off, or do some cross-training which will help you stay in shape without aggravating your injury. And if the pain is severe, or persists more than a few days, see your doctor.

Treating injuries

The basic treatment for most joint and muscle injuries is pretty similar, regardless of the cause. The standard RICE regimen is the place to start:

- ✔ **R is for rest.** Stay off it — that means no weight-bearing exercises. Some recent research suggests that gentle, range-of-motion exercise can speed healing — call this active rest.

- ✔ **I is for Ice.** As soon as possible, put an ice pack on the affected area to keep down swelling and inflammation during the first 48 hours after an acute injury. Icing after exercise can help reduce pain and inflammation of an overuse injury.

- ✔ **C is for compression.** Wrap the joint to keep down the swelling and inflammation. In the case of an acute injury, it means not taking off a shoe or a glove or a pair of tights until you can get home to ice it. If it's an overuse injury, wrapping the area can provide support as well as help reduce pain and inflammation.

- ✔ **E is for elevation.** Raise the affected body part to keep the swelling down.

After checking with your doctor, you can augment the RICE regimen by taking a non-prescription-strength anti-inflammatory (such as Ibuprofen). Anti-inflammatories cannot only ease the pain of injuries and muscle and joint soreness, but also, more importantly, they can actually help promote healing by reducing swelling.

Part II
The Triathlete's Training Diary

The 5th Wave   By Rich Tennant

"Listen, thanks. I'll return them as soon as I get the wheels fixed."

In this part . . .

Got your pen? Great. Because this is the part of the book that you write. The training diary pages in this section are your tabula rasa, a blank slate just waiting for you to record your goals, your accomplishments, and whatever else you'd like to put down on paper.

Date:

Training	Time/Distance	Sets	Reps

Food for Thought

_____

_____

_____

Date:

Training	Time/Distance	Sets	Reps

Food for Thought

_____

_____

_____

Workout Wrap-Up

Accomplishments!   Notes

_____   _____

_____   _____

_____   _____

_____   _____

_____   _____

_____   _____

_____   _____

"When I'm 80, I don't want to look back on my life and just be able to recite the films and the movies and the series that I did."

— former "Baywatch" star Alexandra Paul, on why she competed in the Ironman triathlon

Training Goals

Goals!

_____
_____
_____
_____
_____

....

Date: [_____]

Training	Time/Distance	Sets	Reps
_____	_____	☐	☐
_____	_____	☐	☐
_____	_____	☐	☐
_____	_____	☐	☐
_____	_____	☐	☐

Food for Thought

_____
_____
_____

....

Date: [_____]

Training	Time/Distance	Sets	Reps
_____	_____	☐	☐
_____	_____	☐	☐
_____	_____	☐	☐
_____	_____	☐	☐
_____	_____	☐	☐

Food for Thought

_____
_____
_____

Date:

Training   Time/Distance   Sets Reps

_____

_____

_____

_____

_____

Food for Thought

_____

_____

_____

....

Date:

Training   Time/Distance   Sets Reps

_____

_____

_____

_____

_____

Food for Thought

_____

_____

_____

....

Date:

Training   Time/Distance   Sets Reps

_____

_____

_____

_____

_____

Food for Thought

_____

_____

_____

Date:

Training	Time/Distance	Sets	Reps

Food for Thought

Date:

Training	Time/Distance	Sets	Reps

Food for Thought

Date:

Training	Time/Distance	Sets	Reps

Food for Thought

Date:

Training	Time/Distance	Sets	Reps

Food for Thought

....

Date:

Training	Time/Distance	Sets	Reps

Food for Thought

Workout Wrap-Up

Accomplishments!	Notes

"I believe that every human has a finite number of heartbeats. I don't intend to waste any of mine running around doing exercises."
— Neil Armstrong, retired astronaut, first man on the moon

Training Goals

Goals!

_____

_____

_____

_____

_____

....

Date: [   ]

Training	Time/Distance	Sets	Reps
_____	_____	▢	▢
_____	_____	▢	▢
_____	_____	▢	▢
_____	_____	▢	▢
_____	_____	▢	▢

Food for Thought

_____

_____

_____

....

Date: [   ]

Training	Time/Distance	Sets	Reps
_____	_____	▢	▢
_____	_____	▢	▢
_____	_____	▢	▢
_____	_____	▢	▢
_____	_____	▢	▢

Food for Thought

_____

_____

_____

Date:

Training	Time/Distance	Sets	Reps

Food for Thought

....

Date:

Training	Time/Distance	Sets	Reps

Food for Thought

....

Date:

Training	Time/Distance	Sets	Reps

Food for Thought

Date:

Training	Time/Distance	Sets	Reps

_____

Food for Thought

_____

....

Date:

Training	Time/Distance	Sets	Reps

_____

Food for Thought

_____

....

Date:

Training	Time/Distance	Sets	Reps

_____

Food for Thought

_____

Date:

Training	Time/Distance	Sets	Reps

Food for Thought

....

Date:

Training	Time/Distance	Sets	Reps

Food for Thought

Workout Wrap-Up

Accomplishments!   Notes

"We do not want in the United States a nation of spectators. We want a nation of participants in the vigorous life."
— John F. Kennedy, 35th president of the United States

Training Goals

Goals!

Date:

Training	Time/Distance	Sets	Reps

Food for Thought

Date:

Training	Time/Distance	Sets	Reps

Food for Thought

Date:

Training   Time/Distance   Sets   Reps

_____

_____

_____

_____

_____

Food for Thought

_____

_____

_____

Date:

Training   Time/Distance   Sets   Reps

_____

_____

_____

_____

_____

Food for Thought

_____

_____

_____

Date:

Training   Time/Distance   Sets   Reps

_____

_____

_____

_____

_____

Food for Thought

_____

_____

_____

Date:

Training	Time/Distance	Sets	Reps

Food for Thought

- -

Date:

Training	Time/Distance	Sets	Reps

Food for Thought

- -

Date:

Training	Time/Distance	Sets	Reps

Food for Thought

Date:

Training	Time/Distance	Sets	Reps

Food for Thought

....

Date:

Training	Time/Distance	Sets	Reps

Food for Thought

Workout Wrap-Up

Accomplishments!	Notes

Training Goals

Goals!

_____

_____

_____

_____

_____

....

Date: [   ]

Training	Time/Distance	Sets	Reps
_____	_____		
_____	_____		
_____	_____		
_____	_____		
_____	_____		

Food for Thought

_____

_____

_____

....

Date: [   ]

Training	Time/Distance	Sets	Reps
_____	_____		
_____	_____		
_____	_____		
_____	_____		
_____	_____		

Food for Thought

_____

_____

_____

Date:

Training	Time/Distance	Sets	Reps

Food for Thought

Date:

Training	Time/Distance	Sets	Reps

Food for Thought

Date:

Training	Time/Distance	Sets	Reps

Food for Thought

Date:

Training   Time/Distance   Sets   Reps

_____

_____

_____

_____

_____

Food for Thought

_____

_____

_____

....

Date:

Training   Time/Distance   Sets   Reps

_____

_____

_____

_____

_____

Food for Thought

_____

_____

_____

....

Date:

Training   Time/Distance   Sets   Reps

_____

_____

_____

_____

_____

Food for Thought

_____

_____

_____

Date:

Training	Time/Distance	Sets	Reps

Food for Thought

....

Date:

Training	Time/Distance	Sets	Reps

Food for Thought

Workout Wrap-Up

Accomplishments!	Notes

TIP

"It is almost impossible to be positive about training while being negative about most other aspects of your life."
— *David Whitsett, author of*
The Non-Runners Marathon Trainer

Training Goals

Goals!

_____
_____
_____
_____
_____

Date: [   ]

Training	Time/Distance	Sets	Reps
_____	_____		
_____	_____		
_____	_____		
_____	_____		
_____	_____		

Food for Thought

_____
_____
_____

Date: [   ]

Training	Time/Distance	Sets	Reps
_____	_____		
_____	_____		
_____	_____		
_____	_____		
_____	_____		

Food for Thought

_____
_____
_____

Date:

Training	Time/Distance	Sets	Reps
_____	_____	☐	☐
_____	_____	☐	☐
_____	_____	☐	☐
_____	_____	☐	☐
_____	_____	☐	☐

Food for Thought

_____

_____

_____

....

Date:

Training	Time/Distance	Sets	Reps
_____	_____	☐	☐
_____	_____	☐	☐
_____	_____	☐	☐
_____	_____	☐	☐
_____	_____	☐	☐

Food for Thought

_____

_____

_____

....

Date:

Training	Time/Distance	Sets	Reps
_____	_____	☐	☐
_____	_____	☐	☐
_____	_____	☐	☐
_____	_____	☐	☐
_____	_____	☐	☐

Food for Thought

_____

_____

_____

Date:

Training	Time/Distance	Sets	Reps

Food for Thought

....

Date:

Training	Time/Distance	Sets	Reps

Food for Thought

....

Date:

Training	Time/Distance	Sets	Reps

Food for Thought

Date:

Training	Time/Distance	Sets	Reps

Food for Thought

....

Date:

Training	Time/Distance	Sets	Reps

Food for Thought

Workout Wrap-Up

Accomplishments!   Notes

"I'm never going to live in a nursing home."
— Jim Ward, oldest finisher of Hawaii's Ironman triathlon at the
age of 77, who died at age 83 of an apparent heart attack
during a 72-mile training ride

Training Goals

Goals!

_____

_____

_____

_____

_____

Date: [   ]

Training	Time/Distance	Sets	Reps

Food for Thought

_____

_____

_____

Date: [   ]

Training	Time/Distance	Sets	Reps

Food for Thought

_____

_____

_____

Date:

Training	Time/Distance	Sets	Reps

Food for Thought

....

Date:

Training	Time/Distance	Sets	Reps

Food for Thought

....

Date:

Training	Time/Distance	Sets	Reps

Food for Thought

Date:

Training	Time/Distance	Sets	Reps

Food for Thought

Date:

Training	Time/Distance	Sets	Reps

Food for Thought

Date:

Training	Time/Distance	Sets	Reps

Food for Thought

Date:

Training	Time/Distance	Sets	Reps

Food for Thought

....

Date:

Training	Time/Distance	Sets	Reps

Food for Thought

Workout Wrap-Up

Accomplishments!   Notes

"Avoid running at all times. Don't look back. Something may be gaining on you."

— *Leroy "Satchel" Paige, Hall of Fame pitcher*

Training Goals

Goals!

_____
_____
_____
_____
_____

Date: [　　　　　　]

Training	Time/Distance	Sets	Reps
_____	_____	▢	▢
_____	_____	▢	▢
_____	_____	▢	▢
_____	_____	▢	▢
_____	_____	▢	▢

Food for Thought

_____
_____
_____

Date: [　　　　　　]

Training	Time/Distance	Sets	Reps
_____	_____	▢	▢
_____	_____	▢	▢
_____	_____	▢	▢
_____	_____	▢	▢
_____	_____	▢	▢

Food for Thought

_____
_____
_____

Date:

Training   Time/Distance   Sets   Reps

_____

_____

_____

_____

_____

Food for Thought

_____

_____

_____

....

Date:

Training   Time/Distance   Sets   Reps

_____

_____

_____

_____

_____

Food for Thought

_____

_____

_____

....

Date:

Training   Time/Distance   Sets   Reps

_____

_____

_____

_____

_____

Food for Thought

_____

_____

_____

Date:

Training	Time/Distance	Sets	Reps

Food for Thought

Date:

Training	Time/Distance	Sets	Reps

Food for Thought

Date:

Training	Time/Distance	Sets	Reps

Food for Thought

Date:

Training	Time/Distance	Sets	Reps

Food for Thought

_____

_____

_____

Date:

Training	Time/Distance	Sets	Reps

Food for Thought

_____

_____

_____

Workout Wrap-Up

Accomplishments!	Notes

REMEMBER

"He may win the race that runs by himself."
— *Benjamin Franklin, writer and inventor*

Training Goals

Goals!

_____
_____
_____
_____
_____

Date: [_____]

Training	Time/Distance	Sets	Reps
_____	_____	☐	☐
_____	_____	☐	☐
_____	_____	☐	☐
_____	_____	☐	☐
_____	_____	☐	☐

Food for Thought

_____
_____
_____

Date: [_____]

Training	Time/Distance	Sets	Reps
_____	_____	☐	☐
_____	_____	☐	☐
_____	_____	☐	☐
_____	_____	☐	☐
_____	_____	☐	☐

Food for Thought

_____
_____
_____

Date:

Training   Time/Distance   Sets   Reps

_____

_____

_____

_____

_____

Food for Thought

_____

_____

_____

Date:

Training   Time/Distance   Sets   Reps

_____

_____

_____

_____

_____

Food for Thought

_____

_____

_____

Date:

Training   Time/Distance   Sets   Reps

_____

_____

_____

_____

_____

Food for Thought

_____

_____

_____

Date:

Training	Time/Distance	Sets	Reps

Food for Thought

....

Date:

Training	Time/Distance	Sets	Reps

Food for Thought

....

Date:

Training	Time/Distance	Sets	Reps

Food for Thought

Date:

Training   Time/Distance   Sets Reps

_____   ▢   ▢
_____   ▢   ▢
_____   ▢   ▢
_____   ▢   ▢
_____   ▢   ▢

Food for Thought

_____
_____
_____

Date:

Training   Time/Distance   Sets Reps

_____   ▢   ▢
_____   ▢   ▢
_____   ▢   ▢
_____   ▢   ▢
_____   ▢   ▢

Food for Thought

_____
_____
_____

Workout Wrap-Up

Accomplishments!   Notes

_____   _____
_____   _____
_____   _____
_____   _____
_____   _____
_____   _____
_____   _____
_____   _____

TIP

"There is a time to run and there is a time to rest. It is the true test of the runner to get them both right."
— *Noel Carroll, Irish Olympian*

Training Goals

Goals!

_____
_____
_____
_____
_____

Date: _____

Training	Time/Distance	Sets	Reps

Food for Thought

_____
_____
_____

Date: _____

Training	Time/Distance	Sets	Reps

Food for Thought

_____
_____
_____

Date:

Training	Time/Distance	Sets	Reps
_____	_____	▢	▢
_____	_____	▢	▢
_____	_____	▢	▢
_____	_____	▢	▢
_____	_____	▢	▢

Food for Thought

_____
_____
_____

....

Date:

Training	Time/Distance	Sets	Reps
_____	_____	▢	▢
_____	_____	▢	▢
_____	_____	▢	▢
_____	_____	▢	▢
_____	_____	▢	▢

Food for Thought

_____
_____
_____

....

Date:

Training	Time/Distance	Sets	Reps
_____	_____	▢	▢
_____	_____	▢	▢
_____	_____	▢	▢
_____	_____	▢	▢
_____	_____	▢	▢

Food for Thought

_____
_____
_____

Date:

Training	Time/Distance	Sets	Reps

Food for Thought

....

Date:

Training	Time/Distance	Sets	Reps

Food for Thought

....

Date:

Training	Time/Distance	Sets	Reps

Food for Thought

Date:

Training	Time/Distance	Sets	Reps

Food for Thought

....

Date:

Training	Time/Distance	Sets	Reps

Food for Thought

Workout Wrap-Up

Accomplishments!   Notes

REMEMBER

"If I'd known I was gonna live this long, I'd have taken better care of myself."

— *Eubie Blake, jazz pianist, at age 100*

Training Goals

Goals!

_____

_____

_____

_____

_____

Date: _____

Training	Time/Distance	Sets	Reps
_____	_____	☐	☐
_____	_____	☐	☐
_____	_____	☐	☐
_____	_____	☐	☐
_____	_____	☐	☐

Food for Thought

_____

_____

_____

Date: _____

Training	Time/Distance	Sets	Reps
_____	_____	☐	☐
_____	_____	☐	☐
_____	_____	☐	☐
_____	_____	☐	☐
_____	_____	☐	☐

Food for Thought

_____

_____

_____

Date:

Training	Time/Distance	Sets	Reps

Food for Thought

Date:

Training	Time/Distance	Sets	Reps

Food for Thought

Date:

Training	Time/Distance	Sets	Reps

Food for Thought

Date:

Training	Time/Distance	Sets	Reps

Food for Thought

Date:

Training	Time/Distance	Sets	Reps

Food for Thought

Date:

Training	Time/Distance	Sets	Reps

Food for Thought

Date:

Training	Time/Distance	Sets	Reps

Food for Thought

....

Date:

Training	Time/Distance	Sets	Reps

Food for Thought

Workout Wrap-Up

Accomplishments!	Notes

TIP

"If a man coaches himself, then he has only himself to blame when he is beaten."
— *Roger Bannister, first man to break the four-minute mile*

Training Goals

Goals!

_____

_____

_____

_____

_____

Date: [   ]

Training   Time/Distance   Sets   Reps

_____

_____

_____

_____

_____

Food for Thought

_____

_____

_____

Date: [   ]

Training   Time/Distance   Sets   Reps

_____

_____

_____

_____

_____

Food for Thought

_____

_____

_____

Date:

Training	Time/Distance	Sets	Reps

Food for Thought

Date:

Training	Time/Distance	Sets	Reps

Food for Thought

Date:

Training	Time/Distance	Sets	Reps

Food for Thought

Date:

Training   Time/Distance   Sets   Reps

_____
_____
_____
_____
_____

Food for Thought

_____
_____
_____

....

Date:

Training   Time/Distance   Sets   Reps

_____
_____
_____
_____
_____

Food for Thought

_____
_____
_____

....

Date:

Training   Time/Distance   Sets   Reps

_____
_____
_____
_____
_____

Food for Thought

_____
_____
_____

Date:

Training	Time/Distance	Sets	Reps

Food for Thought

Date:

Training	Time/Distance	Sets	Reps

Food for Thought

Workout Wrap-Up

Accomplishments!	Notes

TIP

"I cannot believe that our muscular vigor will ever be a super-fluity. Even if the day ever dawns in which it will not be needed for fighting the old heavy battles against Nature, it will always be needed to furnish the background of sanity, serenity and cheer-fulness to life, to give moral elasticity to our disposition, to round off the wiry edge of our fretfulness, and make us good humored and easy of approach."

— William James, American philosopher

Training Goals

Goals!

_____
_____
_____

Date: [   ]

Training   Time/Distance   Sets   Reps

_____
_____
_____
_____
_____

Food for Thought

_____
_____
_____

Date: [   ]

Training   Time/Distance   Sets   Reps

_____
_____
_____
_____
_____

Food for Thought

_____
_____
_____

Date:

Training	Time/Distance	Sets	Reps

Food for Thought

....

Date:

Training	Time/Distance	Sets	Reps

Food for Thought

....

Date:

Training	Time/Distance	Sets	Reps

Food for Thought

Date:

Training	Time/Distance	Sets	Reps

Food for Thought

_____
_____
_____

Date:

Training	Time/Distance	Sets	Reps

Food for Thought

_____
_____
_____

Date:

Training	Time/Distance	Sets	Reps

Food for Thought

_____
_____
_____

Date:

Training	Time/Distance	Sets	Reps

Food for Thought

Date:

Training	Time/Distance	Sets	Reps

Food for Thought

Workout Wrap-Up

Accomplishments!	Notes

"I did a half-Ironman in 1984 and I almost drowned. I can't swim. After that I got hit by a car on my bike and I damaged my arm pretty badly and I couldn't swim at all. My bike was destroyed. So I started just running."
— *Ultramarathoner Ann Trason*

Training Goals

Goals!

Date:

Training	Time/Distance	Sets	Reps

Food for Thought

Date:

Training	Time/Distance	Sets	Reps

Food for Thought

Date:

Training   Time/Distance   Sets   Reps

_____

_____

_____

_____

_____

Food for Thought

_____

_____

_____

....

Date:

Training   Time/Distance   Sets   Reps

_____

_____

_____

_____

_____

Food for Thought

_____

_____

_____

....

Date:

Training   Time/Distance   Sets   Reps

_____

_____

_____

_____

_____

Food for Thought

_____

_____

_____

Date:

Training	Time/Distance	Sets	Reps

Food for Thought

....

Date:

Training	Time/Distance	Sets	Reps

Food for Thought

....

Date:

Training	Time/Distance	Sets	Reps

Food for Thought

Date:

Training	Time/Distance	Sets	Reps

Food for Thought

....

Date:

Training	Time/Distance	Sets	Reps

Food for Thought

Workout Wrap-Up

Accomplishments!	Notes

"Exercise is bunk. If you are healthy, you don't need it; if you are sick, you shouldn't take it."

— Henry Ford

Training Goals
Goals!

_____

_____

_____

_____

_____

Date: [   ]

Training	Time/Distance	Sets	Reps
_____	_____		
_____	_____		
_____	_____		
_____	_____		
_____	_____		

Food for Thought

_____

_____

_____

Date: [   ]

Training	Time/Distance	Sets	Reps
_____	_____		
_____	_____		
_____	_____		
_____	_____		
_____	_____		

Food for Thought

_____

_____

_____

Date:

Training	Time/Distance	Sets	Reps

Food for Thought

....

Date:

Training	Time/Distance	Sets	Reps

Food for Thought

....

Date:

Training	Time/Distance	Sets	Reps

Food for Thought

Date:

Training	Time/Distance	Sets	Reps

Food for Thought

....

Date:

Training	Time/Distance	Sets	Reps

Food for Thought

....

Date:

Training	Time/Distance	Sets	Reps

Food for Thought

Date:

Training	Time/Distance	Sets	Reps

Food for Thought

....

Date:

Training	Time/Distance	Sets	Reps

Food for Thought

Workout Wrap-Up

Accomplishments!	Notes

"Take care of your body with steadfast fidelity. The soul must see through these eyes alone, and if they are dim, the whole world is clouded."

— J. W. Goethe, poet and dramatist

Training Goals

Goals!

_____

_____

_____

_____

_____

....

Date: [   ]

Training	Time/Distance	Sets	Reps

Food for Thought

_____

_____

_____

....

Date: [   ]

Training	Time/Distance	Sets	Reps

Food for Thought

_____

_____

_____

Date:

Training	Time/Distance	Sets	Reps

Food for Thought

....

Date:

Training	Time/Distance	Sets	Reps

Food for Thought

....

Date:

Training	Time/Distance	Sets	Reps

Food for Thought

Date:

Training	Time/Distance	Sets	Reps

Food for Thought

_____

_____

_____

....

Date:

Training	Time/Distance	Sets	Reps

Food for Thought

_____

_____

_____

....

Date:

Training	Time/Distance	Sets	Reps

Food for Thought

_____

_____

_____

Date:

Training	Time/Distance	Sets	Reps

Food for Thought

_____
_____
_____

....

Date:

Training	Time/Distance	Sets	Reps

Food for Thought

_____
_____
_____

Workout Wrap-Up

Accomplishments!	Notes

"The brain recalls just what the muscles grope for; no more, no less."

— William Faulkner, Nobel Prize winner in Literature

Training Goals
Goals!

_____
_____
_____
_____
_____

Date: _____

Training	Time/Distance	Sets	Reps
_____	_____		
_____			
_____			
_____			
_____			

Food for Thought

_____
_____
_____

Date: _____

Training	Time/Distance	Sets	Reps
_____	_____		
_____			
_____			
_____			
_____			

Food for Thought

_____
_____
_____

Date:

Training	Time/Distance	Sets	Reps

Food for Thought

Date:

Training	Time/Distance	Sets	Reps

Food for Thought

Date:

Training	Time/Distance	Sets	Reps

Food for Thought

Date:

Training	Time/Distance	Sets	Reps

Food for Thought

Date:

Training	Time/Distance	Sets	Reps

Food for Thought

Date:

Training	Time/Distance	Sets	Reps

Food for Thought

Date:

Training	Time/Distance	Sets	Reps

Food for Thought

_____

_____

_____

Date:

Training	Time/Distance	Sets	Reps

Food for Thought

_____

_____

_____

Workout Wrap-Up

Accomplishments!	Notes

"'What's that little thing floating. Oh, my God, they swam over Robin. Quick. Call David Hasselhoff. It's Baywatch in the water getting Robin out.' I do the bike ride. I love riding bikes."
— Robin Williams, actor, on why he skips the swim leg in the team triathlons he competes in

Training Goals
Goals!

_____
_____
_____
_____
_____

....

Date: _____

Training	Time/Distance	Sets	Reps

Food for Thought
_____
_____
_____

....

Date: _____

Training	Time/Distance	Sets	Reps

Food for Thought
_____
_____
_____

Date:

Training	Time/Distance	Sets	Reps
_____	_____		
_____	_____		
_____	_____		
_____	_____		
_____	_____		

Food for Thought

_____

_____

_____

· ·

Date:

Training	Time/Distance	Sets	Reps
_____	_____		
_____	_____		
_____	_____		
_____	_____		
_____	_____		

Food for Thought

_____

_____

_____

· ·

Date:

Training	Time/Distance	Sets	Reps
_____	_____		
_____	_____		
_____	_____		
_____	_____		
_____	_____		

Food for Thought

_____

_____

_____

Date:

Training	Time/Distance	Sets	Reps

Food for Thought

Date:

Training	Time/Distance	Sets	Reps

Food for Thought

Date:

Training	Time/Distance	Sets	Reps

Food for Thought

Date:

Training	Time/Distance	Sets	Reps

Food for Thought

Date:

Training	Time/Distance	Sets	Reps

Food for Thought

Workout Wrap-Up

Accomplishments!	Notes

Training Goals

Goals!

_____
_____
_____
_____
_____

Date: _____

Training	Time/Distance	Sets	Reps
_____			
_____			
_____			
_____			
_____			

Food for Thought

_____
_____
_____

Date: _____

Training	Time/Distance	Sets	Reps
_____			
_____			
_____			
_____			
_____			

Food for Thought

_____
_____
_____

Date:

Training	Time/Distance	Sets	Reps

Food for Thought

....

Date:

Training	Time/Distance	Sets	Reps

Food for Thought

....

Date:

Training	Time/Distance	Sets	Reps

Food for Thought

Date:

Training	Time/Distance	Sets	Reps

Food for Thought

Date:

Training	Time/Distance	Sets	Reps

Food for Thought

Date:

Training	Time/Distance	Sets	Reps

Food for Thought

Date:

Training	Time/Distance	Sets	Reps

Food for Thought

....

Date:

Training	Time/Distance	Sets	Reps

Food for Thought

Workout Wrap-Up

Accomplishments!   Notes

Training Goals

Goals!

_____
_____
_____
_____
_____

....

Date: _____

Training	Time/Distance	Sets	Reps
_____			
_____			
_____			
_____			
_____			

Food for Thought

_____
_____
_____

....

Date: _____

Training	Time/Distance	Sets	Reps
_____			
_____			
_____			
_____			
_____			

Food for Thought

_____
_____
_____

Date:

Training	Time/Distance	Sets	Reps
_____			
_____			
_____			
_____			
_____			

Food for Thought

_____

_____

_____

Date:

Training	Time/Distance	Sets	Reps
_____			
_____			
_____			
_____			
_____			

Food for Thought

_____

_____

_____

Date:

Training	Time/Distance	Sets	Reps
_____			
_____			
_____			
_____			
_____			

Food for Thought

_____

_____

_____

Date:

Training	Time/Distance	Sets	Reps

Food for Thought

Date:

Training	Time/Distance	Sets	Reps

Food for Thought

Date:

Training	Time/Distance	Sets	Reps

Food for Thought

Date:

Training	Time/Distance	Sets	Rep

Food for Thought

_____

_____

Date:

Training	Time/Distance	Sets	Reps

Food for Thought

_____

_____

_____

Workout Wrap-Up

Accomplishments!	Notes

> *"If I was the shark, I'd be scared."*
> *— Lokelani McMichael, who at 18 was the youngest finisher of the Ironman triathlon, on the possibility of shark attacks during the race*

Training Goals

Goals!

_____
_____
_____
_____
_____

....

Date: [   ]

Training   Time/Distance   Sets   Reps

_____
_____
_____
_____
_____

Food for Thought

_____
_____
_____

....

Date: [   ]

Training   Time/Distance   Sets   Reps

_____
_____
_____
_____
_____

Food for Thought

_____
_____
_____

Date:

Training	Time/Distance	Sets	Reps

Food for Thought

....

Date:

Training	Time/Distance	Sets	Reps

Food for Thought

....

Date:

Training	Time/Distance	Sets	Reps

Food for Thought

Date:

Training   Time/Distance   Sets   Reps

_____

_____

_____

_____

_____

Food for Thought

_____

_____

_____

....

Date:

Training   Time/Distance   Sets   Reps

_____

_____

_____

_____

_____

Food for Thought

_____

_____

_____

....

Date:

Training   Time/Distance   Sets   Reps

_____

_____

_____

_____

_____

Food for Thought

_____

_____

_____

Date:

Training	Time/Distance	Sets	Reps

Food for Thought

....

Date:

Training	Time/Distance	Sets	Reps

Food for Thought

Workout Wrap-Up

Accomplishments!   Notes

REMEMBER

"The sovereign invigorator of the body is exercise, and of all the exercises walking is the best."

— Thomas Jefferson,
American statesman and 3rd president of the United States

Training Goals

Goals!

_____

_____

_____

_____

_____

Date: [   ]

Training   Time/Distance   Sets   Reps

_____

_____

_____

_____

_____

Food for Thought

_____

_____

_____

Date: [   ]

Training   Time/Distance   Sets   Reps

_____

_____

_____

_____

_____

Food for Thought

_____

_____

_____

Date:

Training	Time/Distance	Sets	Reps

Food for Thought

....

Date:

Training	Time/Distance	Sets	Reps

Food for Thought

....

Date:

Training	Time/Distance	Sets	Reps

Food for Thought

Date:

Training	Time/Distance	Sets	Reps

Food for Thought

Date:

Training	Time/Distance	Sets	Reps

Food for Thought

Date:

Training	Time/Distance	Sets	Reps

Food for Thought

Date:

Training	Time/Distance	Sets	Reps

Food for Thought

....

Date:

Training	Time/Distance	Sets	Reps

Food for Thought

Workout Wrap-Up

Accomplishments!   Notes

"People say I've given people courage. That makes me feel good, but I don't see how I do that. I think my running is a selfish thing. But it provides the challenge that allows me to feel good about myself. How can I expect to do well in other activities if I don't feel good about myself?"
— *Joan Benoit, Olympic Marathon champion*

Training Goals

Goals!

_____

_____

_____

_____

_____

Date: [   ]

Training	Time/Distance	Sets	Reps
_____	_____	☐	☐
_____	_____	☐	☐
_____	_____	☐	☐
_____	_____	☐	☐
_____	_____	☐	☐

Food for Thought

_____

_____

_____

Date: [   ]

Training	Time/Distance	Sets	Reps
_____	_____	☐	☐
_____	_____	☐	☐
_____	_____	☐	☐
_____	_____	☐	☐
_____	_____	☐	☐

Food for Thought

_____

_____

_____

Date:

Training	Time/Distance	Sets	Reps
_____	_____		
_____	_____		
_____	_____		
_____	_____		
_____	_____		

Food for Thought

_____

_____

_____

Date:

Training	Time/Distance	Sets	Reps
_____	_____		
_____	_____		
_____	_____		
_____	_____		
_____	_____		

Food for Thought

_____

_____

_____

Date:

Training	Time/Distance	Sets	Reps
_____	_____		
_____	_____		
_____	_____		
_____	_____		
_____	_____		

Food for Thought

_____

_____

_____

Date:

Training	Time/Distance	Sets	Reps

Food for Thought

Date:

Training	Time/Distance	Sets	Reps

Food for Thought

Date:

Training	Time/Distance	Sets	Reps

Food for Thought

Date:

Training	Time/Distance	Sets	Reps

Food for Thought

. . . .

Date:

Training	Time/Distance	Sets	Reps

Food for Thought

Workout Wrap-Up

Accomplishments!	Notes

"A pint of sweat saves a gallon of blood."
— George Patton, U.S. Army General

Training Goals

Goals!

Training	Time/Distance	Sets	Reps

Food for Thought

Date:

Training	Time/Distance	Sets	Reps

Food for Thought

Date:

Training	Time/Distance	Sets	Reps

Food for Thought

....

Date:

Training	Time/Distance	Sets	Reps

Food for Thought

....

Date:

Training	Time/Distance	Sets	Reps

Food for Thought

Date:

Training   Time/Distance   Sets   Reps

_____
_____
_____
_____
_____

Food for Thought

_____
_____
_____

Date:

Training   Time/Distance   Sets   Reps

_____
_____
_____
_____
_____

Food for Thought

_____
_____
_____

Date:

Training   Time/Distance   Sets   Reps

_____
_____
_____
_____
_____

Food for Thought

_____
_____
_____

Date:

Training	Time/Distance	Sets	Reps

Food for Thought

_____

_____

_____

Date:

Training	Time/Distance	Sets	Reps

Food for Thought

_____

_____

_____

Workout Wrap-Up

Accomplishments!	Notes

"Slow running just makes you a slow runner."
—Grete Waitz, nine-time winner
of the New York City Marathon

Training Goals

Goals!

_____
_____
_____
_____
_____

Date: [   ]

Training	Time/Distance	Sets	Reps
_____	_____		
_____	_____		
_____	_____		
_____	_____		
_____	_____		

Food for Thought

_____
_____
_____

Date: [   ]

Training	Time/Distance	Sets	Reps
_____	_____		
_____	_____		
_____	_____		
_____	_____		
_____	_____		

Food for Thought

_____
_____
_____

Date:

Training	Time/Distance	Sets	Reps

Food for Thought

....

Date:

Training	Time/Distance	Sets	Reps

Food for Thought

....

Date:

Training	Time/Distance	Sets	Reps

Food for Thought

Date:

Training   Time/Distance   Sets   Reps

_____

_____

_____

_____

_____

Food for Thought

_____

_____

_____

....

Date:

Training   Time/Distance   Sets   Reps

_____

_____

_____

_____

_____

Food for Thought

_____

_____

_____

....

Date:

Training   Time/Distance   Sets   Reps

_____

_____

_____

_____

_____

Food for Thought

_____

_____

_____

Date:

Training	Time/Distance	Sets	Reps

Food for Thought

_____

_____

_____

....

Date:

Training	Time/Distance	Sets	Reps

Food for Thought

_____

_____

_____

Workout Wrap-Up

Accomplishments!	Notes

"Now my task is smoothly done/I can fly or I can run."
— John Milton, writer

Training Goals
Goals!

_____
_____
_____
_____
_____

Date: [   ]

Training	Time/Distance	Sets	Reps
_____	_____		
_____	_____		
_____	_____		
_____	_____		
_____	_____		

Food for Thought
_____
_____
_____

Date: [   ]

Training	Time/Distance	Sets	Reps
_____	_____		
_____	_____		
_____	_____		
_____	_____		
_____	_____		

Food for Thought
_____
_____
_____

Date:

Training   Time/Distance   Sets   Reps

_____

_____

_____

_____

_____

Food for Thought

_____

_____

_____

Date:

Training   Time/Distance   Sets   Reps

_____

_____

_____

_____

_____

Food for Thought

_____

_____

_____

Date:

Training   Time/Distance   Sets   Reps

_____

_____

_____

_____

_____

Food for Thought

_____

_____

_____

Date:

Training   Time/Distance   Sets Reps

_____

_____

_____

_____

_____

Food for Thought

_____

_____

_____

Date:

Training   Time/Distance   Sets Reps

_____

_____

_____

_____

_____

Food for Thought

_____

_____

_____

Date:

Training   Time/Distance   Sets Reps

_____

_____

_____

_____

_____

Food for Thought

_____

_____

_____

Date:

Training   Time/Distance   Sets   Reps

_____

_____

_____

_____

_____

Food for Thought

_____

_____

_____

....

Date:

Training   Time/Distance   Sets   Reps

_____

_____

_____

_____

_____

Food for Thought

_____

_____

_____

Workout Wrap-Up

Accomplishments!   Notes

_____   _____

_____   _____

_____   _____

_____   _____

_____   _____

_____   _____

_____   _____

_____   _____

"In anguish we uplift/A new unhallowed song/The race is to the swift/The battle to the strong"
— *John Davidson, singer and game show host*

Training Goals

Goals!

_____
_____
_____
_____
_____

Date: _____

Training	Time/Distance	Sets	Reps
_____			
_____			
_____			
_____			
_____			

Food for Thought

_____
_____
_____

Date: _____

Training	Time/Distance	Sets	Reps
_____			
_____			
_____			
_____			
_____			

Food for Thought

_____
_____
_____

Date:

Training	Time/Distance	Sets	Reps

Food for Thought

Date:

Training	Time/Distance	Sets	Reps

Food for Thought

Date:

Training	Time/Distance	Sets	Reps

Food for Thought

Date:

Training   Time/Distance   Sets   Reps

_____

_____

_____

_____

_____

Food for Thought

_____

_____

_____

Date:

Training   Time/Distance   Sets   Reps

_____

_____

_____

_____

_____

Food for Thought

_____

_____

_____

Date:

Training   Time/Distance   Sets   Reps

_____

_____

_____

_____

_____

Food for Thought

_____

_____

_____

Date:

Training	Time/Distance	Sets	Reps

Food for Thought

....

Date:

Training	Time/Distance	Sets	Reps

Food for Thought

Workout Wrap-Up

Accomplishments!	Notes

Part III

The Part of Tens

The 5th Wave   By Rich Tennant

"I heard it was good to cross-train, so I'm mixing my weight training with scuba diving."

In this part . . .

Everyone loves a list, right? Well, the Part of Tens pages are like dessert, a few quick tips to help make exercising something that's not only good for you, but fun, too. Think of it as spinach salad with a crème brûlée chaser.

Chapter 5

Ten Things That You Can't Forget on Race Day

*O*n race day, at least a million things will be running through your mind. Post this checklist and at least you won't forget something really essential.

Goggles

If there's one thing that's more challenging than an open water swim, it's an open water swim when you can't see. While you may take on the health club pool without eyewear, you'll be happy you have them once you hit the waves.

Sunscreen

You have enough physical challenges without a sunburn. But remember to wear sports-specific screen, which won't sweat off, and more importantly, won't drip into your eyes and have you squinting through half the bike leg.

Your Bike Helmet

They're required for the bike leg, so if you leave yours at home, your triathlon will be over before it's hardly begun. And just in case of a Murphy's Law scenario — another racer grabs your helmet by accident before you get there — some folks even bring a spare.

Spare Inner Tube

Flats happen, usually at the most inopportune time. And when time is of the essence, it's a lot quicker to whip out a spare tube than to try to patch the holey one. But your spare inner tube won't do much good if you don't have something to pump it up with. A CO_2 inflator will work too, but make sure you're carrying a spare cartridge.

Food

A triathlete doesn't run on willpower alone. So make sure you've packed energy bars, sports gel, or some low-tech fuel like a banana and a few Fig Newtons. Or risk having your race end with a bonk.

Lubrication

Not for your bike, but for you. You might bring Vaseline or even cooking oil spray to apply before the swim so that you can get your wetsuit on more easily. And don't forget the anti-chafing solution of your choice for high friction areas on the bike and the run.

Sunglasses

Not only will your eyes thank you for it — sunglasses fight glare and debris — a good pair will also help hide the grimace during your more difficult moments. In other words, they help you both see and look better.

Your Race Number

It could be worse than getting to the finish line, only to have the person holding the tape shake their head. Your time doesn't count if you don't have a number. And don't forget safety pins to attach it.

Cash

As a guy on a train in Scotland once said to me, "You can't have any fun, if you don't have any mon . . . ." I assume he meant money, and without some, you're not going to be able to buy a post-race meal or even a cab ride back home.

Whatever Else

There's something that's going to make you happy at the start or the finish, and maybe during the race. Is it your lucky baseball cap? Your Walkman? Or your favorite stuffed animal? And don't forget personal necessities, such as contact lenses and prescription medications.

Chapter 6

Ten Ways to Reward Yourself for Finishing a Triathlon

. . . .

In This Chapter

▶ Eating with Ronald McDonald

▶ Pumping up the volume

▶ Treating yourself to a day off

. . . .

*H*owever you may try to convince yourself otherwise before and during the race, running a triathlon is hard work. Here are a variety of ways you can indulge yourself afterwards.

Junk Food

Okay, Peter Reid, you've just won the Ironman Triathlon. Where are you gonna go? To McDonalds. Yup, it's the truth, the Canadian champion went straight from the finish line to the Golden Arches, with his wife — and fellow top triathlete — Lori Bowden in tow.

A Gastronomic Feast

If you're not a large-fries-and-a-shake kind of guy, go for a different kind of gastronomic reward. Make a reservation at the best restaurant in town, start with the foie gras and then go from there. If you can't order crème brulee guilt-free today, when can you?

A Massage

You can convince yourself it's all about getting rid of excess lactic acid and stimulating blood circulation to your aching muscles and joints. But lying on the table, you'll realize that there's nothing quite like the sensual synergy of educated hands and an overworked body.

A Nap

Okay, you haven't slept during daylight since grammar school. You haven't followed a swim with a bike ride and a long run since then either. Yawwwwn . . . .

Music

What better way to chill out or pump yourself up? If you're feeling ambitious, you could construct some theme mixes. Maybe start with Handel's *Water Music,* follow up with Leo Kottke's *Busted Bicycle,* and end the set with Bruce Springsteen's *Born To Run.*

Companionship

One top female triathlete, an age-group winner in the Ironman, finds that it helps her focus to abstain from sex for three days before a race. What does her husband say about this? "He's always waiting for me at the finish line," she smiles.

A Party

What better reason to celebrate than successfully finishing a triathlon? And if you don't plan the celebration, who will? Make it pot luck so that you don't have to worry about shopping or cooking — and emphasize in advance that this will not be a dance party.

A Day Off

Take a vacation day the day after the race. Then you can stay up late, sleep in, and goof off. You can always regale your co-workers with your exploits on Tuesday.

A Movie

What better way to take your mind off a long afternoon in the sun than to escape to an alternate reality inside a darkened theatre? What kind of movie? Anything you want . . . except maybe *Marathon Man.*

A New Toy

Remember how Mom took you toy shopping after you jumped into the deep end of the pool? What better occasion for a little spending splurge than in the wake of a big accomplishment? You remember the old saying: When the going gets tough, the tough go shopping.

Index

• *V* •

vague goals, 11

• *W* •

warm-up
  aerobic exercise, 27
  pre-stretch, 27–28
  stretching, 29–34
watch, 15
water, 57–58
weight training. *See* strength
    training
wetsuit
  lubrication, 184
  transition to cycling and, 41

workouts. *See also* exercise
  building plan, 20, 22
  eating after, 56–57
  eating during, 55–56
  eating prior to, 54
  endurance, 19
  LSD, 19
  rest-and-recovery balance, 13
  schedule setup, 13–14
  sickness and, 33
  speed intervals, 20
  strength training, 19–20
  types, 19–20

Notes

Take the mystery out of exercising right!

Introducing fitness videos for the rest of us!

These un-intimidating exercise videos explain fitness techniques in easy-to-understand language. Not only can you reshape your body with these videos —you may even change your mind about exercise.

Available at retailers everywhere, or by calling (800) 546-1949.

WWW.DUMMIES.COM

YOUR ONLINE RESOURCE

Discover Dummies Online!

The Dummies Web Site is your fun and friendly online resource for the latest information about *For Dummies®* books and your favorite topics. The Web site is the place to communicate with us, exchange ideas with other *For Dummies* readers, chat with authors, and have fun!

Ten Fun and Useful Things You Can Do at www.dummies.com

1. Win free *For Dummies* books and more!
2. Register your book and be entered in a prize drawing.
3. Meet your favorite authors through the IDG Books Worldwide Author Chat Series.
4. Exchange helpful information with other *For Dummies* readers.
5. Discover other great *For Dummies* books you must have!
6. Purchase Dummieswear® exclusively from our Web site.
7. Buy *For Dummies* books online.
8. Talk to us. Make comments, ask questions, get answers!
9. Download free software.
10. Find additional useful resources from authors.

Link directly to these ten fun and useful things at
http://www.dummies.com/10useful

For other technology titles from IDG Books Worldwide, go to
www.idgbooks.com

Not on the Web yet? It's easy to get started with *Dummies 101®: The Internet For Windows® 98* or *The Internet For Dummies®* at local retailers everywhere.

Find other *For Dummies* books on these topics:
Business • Career • Databases • Food & Beverage • Games • Gardening • Graphics • Hardware
Health & Fitness • Internet and the World Wide Web • Networking • Office Suites
Operating Systems • Personal Finance • Pets • Programming • Recreation • Sports
Spreadsheets • Teacher Resources • Test Prep • Word Processing

IDG BOOKS WORLDWIDE BOOK REGISTRATION

Register This Book and Win!

We want to hear from you!

Visit **http://my2cents.dummies.com** to register this book and tell us how you liked it!

- ✔ Get entered in our monthly prize giveaway.

- ✔ Give us feedback about this book — tell us what you like best, what you like least, or maybe what you'd like to ask the author and us to change!

- ✔ Let us know any other *For Dummies®* topics that interest you.

Your feedback helps us determine what books to publish, tells us what coverage to add as we revise our books, and lets us know whether we're meeting your needs as a *For Dummies* reader. You're our most valuable resource, and what you have to say is important to us!

Not on the Web yet? It's easy to get started with *Dummies 101®: The Internet For Windows® 98* or *The Internet For Dummies®* at local retailers everywhere.

Or let us know what you think by sending us a letter at the following address:

For Dummies Book Registration
Dummies Press
10475 Crosspoint Blvd.
Indianapolis, IN 46256

™

**BESTSELLING
BOOK SERIES**